THE ZEN OF IT

PALMETTO

P U B L I S H I N G

Charleston, SC

www.PalmettoPublishing.com

Copyright © 2024 by Andy Cheng | Renato Bellu | Hoag Holmgren

All rights reserved

Hardcover ISBN: 979-8-8229-5763-3
Paperback ISBN: 979-8-8229-5764-0
eBook ISBN: 979-8-8229-5765-7

THE ZEN OF IT

An Enlightened Approach
to Business Software Implementation

Andy Cheng | Renato Bellu | Hoag Holmgren

Preface

Join the Zen of IT revolution.

In this book we share deep insights gained from decades of intimate involvement in innumerable IT projects in a variety of roles at organizations of all types and sizes including educational institutions, public sector governmental agencies, not-for-profit charities, hospitals and clinics, technology startups, family-owned businesses, mid-market companies such as distributors, manufacturers, consulting firms, and staffing companies, as well as large publicly traded multi-national corporations which are household names.

What have we witnessed? What have we learned? What have we endured?

First off, we have seen some really bad things happen to really good people. We have seen people lose their jobs over failed IT projects. We have seen business owners lose millions of dollars out of their own pockets. We have seen corporate officers lose years of precious time as they desperately scrambled to keep up with the technological advances in their industry and fell woefully behind the competition. We have seen very ambitious and well-funded IT projects scrapped after millions of dollars were flushed down the toilet. We have seen morale plummet and employees quit in droves across the entire enterprise as users were forced onto an unstable system. We have seen project managers shocked, dismayed, and then dismissed when, at long last, they came to the stark realization that the IT project that they have been reporting to top management as being on track for the last two years is never going to go live at all and will have to be completely scrapped. We have been called in to perform the autopsies and devise a way forward on multi-million-dollar IT project resets.

Worse yet, we have seen many organizations simply give up, as they reasoned it's just too complicated, expensive, and risky to replace the homegrown spaghetti code octopus that is strangling their organization and stifling their much needed digital transformation. We have seen many companies limping along on ludicrously outdated systems including dreaded green-screen applications that pre-date the advent of Microsoft DOS, much less the advent of the mouse and the graphical user interface. We have seen the frustration of users forced to run their core mission critical processes such as inventory control, purchasing, billing, and logistics using unstable remote desktop sessions connecting to 1980's era client/server applications, applications which cannot talk to all their other apps which are now web portals running happily in an internet browser and connecting them to a vast interconnected ecosystem of suppliers, staffing agencies, couriers, banks, and partner and subsidiary firms, a world cut-off from their core ERP system which is still stuck in the old client/server paradigm.

Many companies have been running the same monolithic software packages for over thirty or even forty years and now, sadly, they are introducing these dinosaur systems to recent college graduates. This is the equivalent of asking your preteen to use a Princess rotary phone hooked into a landline instead of an iPhone to post a pic on Instagram. You wouldn't use such horribly outdated technology to order a pizza, and yet, billion-dollar global organizations with thousands of employees are using old technology for their mission critical functions such as billing, customer service, general ledger, payables, receivables, bank reconciliation, inventory control, purchasing, and logistics. These outdated technologies are kept alive using virtual servers which mimic the antiquated operating systems on which these antique applications run, which amounts to wasting the horsepower of today's optimized computer chips to run yesterday's obsolete apps.

And we have seen paper. Lots of paper. So much paper that it is a wonder that there are any trees left on this planet. Paperless workflow systems have been around for decades, and yet when you go to a business or a doctor's office you are asked to pick up a Bic pen and a clipboard and fill out your name, address, and health plan ID number for the fifth time that day. We have seen the reams of paper and reports still being printed out on old-school dot-matrix printers which require replacement parts to be searched for on eBay when the printer breaks down (as it often does).

But happily, we have also seen victory. We have tasted the sweetness of a new system launch that goes so smoothly, it is referred to as a "boring" go live. We love a boring go live and we know how to achieve it. We have succeeded where others have failed in multiple previous attempts. For example, on one IT project, we replaced a four-decade old mainframe that had been implemented in 1969 by IBM that was still running the mission critical accounting functions for a major US city!

We have seen users empowered by automated integrations who now have the time to analyze information and to serve customers instead of frantically keying, re-keying, double-keying, triple-keying, and endlessly manipulating data in dozens of disconnected loose Microsoft Excel files that suffer from the dreaded problem of "multiple versions of the truth" and require cutting & pasting, pivot tables, filtering, and reformatting before the data can be emailed via an Outlook email attachment to its next stop on the so-called workflow. We have seen the end of paper, the end of using Excel as a database, the end of remote desktop and VPN connections, the end of printing out emails, scanning them, faxing them, and then knowing that some other harried person will end up re-keying that same data into a character-based mainframe dumb terminal.

We have seen an end to the madness.

We have seen enough to know the truth. We have lived, learned, and seen it all, and we know the answer to these questions. We are sharing these answers with you in this book.

We call these answers Core Concepts. There are three Core Concepts:

1. **Embrace Change**
2. **Seek Balance**
3. **Act as One**

Embrace Change covers what to do before you even begin to plan an IT project. Seek Balance covers what you must do at the outset of your project as you formulate a project plan. Lastly, Act as One covers what to do during the execution of the project.

Each Core Concept has three Components.

Embrace Change
Before You Start Planning...

ATTITUDES   POLICIES   DATA

Seek Balance
When Formulating a Plan...

SCOPE   PHASES   ROLES

Act as One
When Executing Your Plan

FOCUS   DESIGN   DOCUMENTATION

The purpose of this book is to share this precious wisdom. And we do so by sharing our war stories in real true-to-life anecdotes as well as by explaining the Core Concepts Components in down-to-earth plain language. This is not a technical treatise which has to adhere to academic formalities. This book is written by hands-on practitioners for people with practical concerns about their upcoming or on-going IT projects.

Unsurprisingly this precious wisdom is mirrored in the principles and teachings of Zen. By understanding Zen principles and how they relate to our Core Concept Components, you will gain our knowledge, and your IT projects will succeed. This book will help you to make a profound positive impact in planning and implementing IT projects of all kinds.

This book is not concerned about appearing hip or in-the-know by using the latest buzzwords. Call it accounting software or ERP (enterprise resource planning) or financial applications, or back-office. Call it CRM (customer relationship management) or customer engagement, sales force automation, or front-office. Call it ECM (enterprise content management) or document management, or document imaging or paperless workflow. Call it reporting, BI (business intelligence) or CPM (corporate performance management). Call it project management or Lean or Agile. It does not matter.

Buzzwords are not magic words. You will not succeed just because you can pronounce the word Agile, or you are hip enough to know that the acronym CPM may now be favored over the acronym BI. The inventors of buzzwords are great at creating new terminology for the same old problem, without solving the problem. Call it reporting or BI or CPM. The question is why is the shipping clerk still printing out a paper report and annotating it with an ink pen as the only means of controlling and organizing shipments at a multi-million-dollar distributor? Why has this inefficient process persisted for the last three decades? Why is there seemingly no end in sight to this inefficiency? The terminology favored by IT pundits changes, but the same old inefficient processes remain. And it's not just replacing paper, of course.

If you are "printing" to PDF file format and saving thousands of unindexed PDF files to a disconnected folder on a laptop hard drive your paper is virtual but your process may very well still be cumbersome, time-consuming, redundant, and inefficient.

Nowadays the prevailing wisdom which is being touted as the ultimate cure-all is more or better project management which means the end of traditional project management and the adoption of Lean and Agile project management. They believe that Lean and Agile are the answer to everything, certainly IT and in fact, the operations of all departments throughout the organization. Lean was developed by Toyota, a car manufacturer, and Agile was adopted by software developers who were looking at how to organize a team of software engineers to program apps. Most organizations are not automobile manufacturers, nor are they software developers. The Lean and Agile methodologies do not make sense for every situation, and yet we have witnessed many evangelists of Lean and Agile awkwardly trying to shoehorn in concepts like bugs, user stories, and features into absolutely every type of business process when clearly these methodologies relate specifically to software development, not for instance, managing a vendor relationship or running a help desk.

While it is true that Lean and Agile are a great step forward in organizational behavior, and you should definitely learn about Lean and Agile methodologies and adopt them in your organization where it makes sense to do so, however, it is not true that the answer to why IT projects fail is the antiquated horrors of traditional waterfall project management as opposed to the divine glory of Lean and Agile. In the past, did ALL IT projects fail? No. Some IT projects failed whereas others succeeded. IT projects are still failing in great numbers, despite the fact that Lean and Agile are being over-adopted everywhere to a ludicrous degree. Every meeting nowadays is labelled a "scrum" or some other hokey term, instead of simply being known as a "meeting". But IT projects are still failing just as much as they always did. Maybe more.

Project management is one aspect, not the whole story.

Lean and Agile methodology is super important, but it is not a cure-all, and it should be adopted only where it makes sense to do so and implemented intelligently. Just running the same old stupid wasteful weekly meeting but now labelling the meeting as a "scrum" instead of a meeting is not adopting Agile methodology, rather it is just batting around buzzwords. Much of so-called Lean and Agile adoption is just that, relabeling the same dysfunctional project management style with the new hip buzzwords.

Lean and Agile teaching is now a huge industry and the purveyors of Lean and Agile are busy making these methodologies more and more complicated and offering more and more advanced certifications in it. This book is an antidote to that kind of needless complexity. In this book we are sharing common sense gained through experience, not simply jumping on the Lean and Agile bandwagon.

Buzzwords and bandwagons will not get users off of inefficient outdated IT systems and onto powerful new efficient cloud-based IT systems. What will work is coming up with a reasonable scope and timeframe and staffing your IT project adequately and tracking the progress of the project intelligently. In this book we go over how to do this. You do this by understanding and incorporating all nine of our Core Concept Components. Please don't make Core Concept Components into the acronym CCC. Instead, absorb this wisdom and use it to make IT systems better.

WHY IT PROJECTS FAIL

There is one overriding reason why IT projects fail. It is not because of faulty project management methodology. It is because people underestimate how entrenched and complex the legacy system is, and they do so because that system is invisible to them. The IT system is not a physical object that takes up space in a building. They cannot see it with their eyes nor touch it with their hands. If they were asked how much time and effort would be required to cut down ten thousand trees as they looked out from atop a high tower over a vast forest, they might give a reasonable answer. Not so with IT systems. We will open up your eyes and teach you to see the entire forest as well as the roots hidden deep beneath the ground.

In this book, we get you to stop underestimating and to start estimating. We don't have to worry about overestimating; overestimating isn't a problem because nobody does it. Over promising and underdelivering should not be the norm in IT, and it doesn't have to be. By absorbing the wisdom contained in this book you will be equipped to be part of a collaborative team that can deliver a production ready IT system, on-schedule, on-budget, every time; you can be part of a gloriously boring go live; you can be part of a revolution in IT systems, pre-planning, planning, and execution. This revolution is the Zen of IT.

WHAT THIS BOOK FOCUSES ON AND WHY

This book focuses on the correct philosophical approach toward the selection, implementation, configuration, adoption, and continuous process improvement of the applications that comprise the core business software of your organization. This book is not about trends in software development, nor coding techniques, nor hardware and network infrastructure, nor artificial intelligence, nor any of the many glamorous and cutting-edge, ultra-technical, and over-hyped information technology topics that most of us are unlikely to actually deal with on a daily basis. This book concerns itself with how to approach the most relevant and important topic related to information technology for most people and most organizations, namely, what are your business policies, what apps are you using, how are those apps tied (or not tied) together, and what business process workflows have you put in place to make the most efficient use of those apps. This book is for a wide audience of people, because everyone in an organization has to deal with the organization's business policies, mix of apps and the various business process workflows that are in place to adhere to and deliver on those polices using those apps, whereas very few people work on creating robots that can pass a Turing test or setting up server farms to mine Bitcoin or other such arcane, albeit glamorous, topics.

Table of Contents

Embrace Change

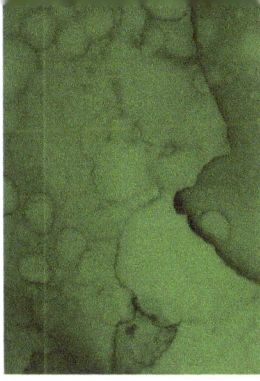

Introduction

There is nothing but change.

Poets, mystics, and sages have been pointing this out for millennia. "You can't step in the same river twice," said Heraclitus over two thousand years ago. The lesser-known philosopher Cratylus amended this a hundred years later by saying "You can't step in the same river once." Yes, the river is never the same river. The person stepping into the river is never the same person.

So, the question is: what is our relationship to change? Can we harness the power of change, like a kayaker paddling skillfully and creatively downstream through the rapids?

Or shall we insist on business as usual, pretending that change is optional, resisting the inevitable, and continue to wade awkwardly and haltingly upstream? "I'm fine," we say, smiling to the onlookers. "It's all good."

How might we manage change more effectively?

When it comes to IT and change, as detailed in the following three chapters, change must not only be managed; it must be embraced.

In Zen training, there is a concept known as wu-wei, inspired by Taoism, and is usually translated as "effortless effort." Wu-wei is based on the observation that it is resistance to change that is the problem, not the change itself.

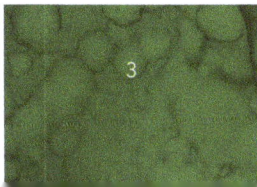

Wu-wei is a core principle in the martial art of Tai Chi, where one trains the body and mind to flow seamlessly from one form to another. It's impossible to say where one form begins and another ends. One simply becomes the embodiment of change. To an experienced Tai Chi practitioner, it is unclear if they are practicing the forms or if the forms are practicing them.

There is a profound economy of effort in wu-wei: nothing extra, nothing lacking. There is only flow. No problem.

But we resist change. Why? Because we like what's familiar. If it's familiar, we're comfortable. We can stay on autopilot and not have to think or reflect or grow or improve. And we often prefer the familiar so much that we would rather suffer profoundly than embrace something new.

Being aware of this very human tendency is the first step to embracing change and finding freedom.

As part of this first step, we might reflect upon how the following questions can clarify the way forward:

- What are we holding onto?
- What are we afraid of losing?
- How can we simplify rules and policies and reporting?
- What are the long-term costs of resistance to change?
- How can we make sure there is top-down buy-in?
- What might be gained if we embrace change?

Change, however, must be intelligent. It must be deliberate, thoroughly planned ahead of time, and well-executed.

As you'll soon see, it's not about a single one-time leap or a "Big Bang" flash where someone flips a switch, and everything changes from grainy black & white to high-definition technicolor.

Zen is known for its simplicity. When washing the dishes, just wash the dishes. Don't get caught up in wishing you were surfing the North Shore instead. When surfing the North Shore, just surf the North Shore. Don't get caught up in wishing that your vacation will never end.

When useless things do not hang in the mind, Every season is your best season.

What can be thrown overboard to lighten the IT load?

What complexities can be streamlined?

What's unnecessary? What's outdated? What's slowing things down?

What's creating extra, unnecessary work?

Simplification must be embraced from within the culture, as part of a new culture from the very beginning; it doesn't start at the end of a project with everyone high-fiving each other like NASA technicians when a lander successfully touches down on Mars. As you'll soon read: "...we MUST simplify our lives BEFORE we can successfully revamp our IT systems."

Zen is also known for its embrace of not-knowing. Not-knowing, it is said, is most intimate. When we know something, there is nothing left to learn. We are shut down and closed off. In the state of not-knowing, we are open, aware, and responsive. We are engaged and alert to opportunity and to the creative quality of change.

What would it look like to embrace change and step forth into a new world?

Change is hard. But change is freedom. Change is life. Change is progress. Change is growth. A failed IT project most often simply means that nothing has changed. Everyone is still stuck on the old inefficient system.

Adopt an attitude of embracing change and spread that attitude across all levels of the organization. Make the people fall in love with the coming changes to the IT system. Do whatever it takes. Bribe them if you have to; create incentives, give promotions, run campaigns, have a party with yummy snacks every Friday, go bowling, hire entertainers, or give away prizes; in short, do whatever it takes to get everyone pumped up and excited about the change. Humans are emotional creatures. An employee sits behind a desk and struggles to keep up with endless emails and a backlog of unprocessed transactions and customer requests. The last thing they want to hear about is that they will have to learn a whole new system. They dread it. They are terrified. They worry that they won't be able to learn the system and they will end up losing their job. They will be out of work and unable to pay the bills. Be sensitive to the very real fears of the end-users down in the trenches.

When you launch your IT project (or the 3rd re-boot of the same old IT project) make change management Job #1. Add a hefty change management component into the IT budget. Stop treating change management as a nice-to-have, when in reality, it's a you-better-freaking-have-it!

But what have we seen?

Most IT Projects do not have any change management to speak of. Even very large multi-million-dollar projects do not contain a change management component. There is generally no budget for any resources to focus on communicating the benefits of the upcoming automation changes and giving them confidence that the proposed new system will indeed become a reality. Many end-users are skeptical that anything will change at all. They have lived through failed attempts in the past. You must have a change management plan and you must act on that plan for swaying the users from the default attitude of fear, dread, and doubt to the much less common attitude of hope, excitement, and confidence.

Changing the attitude of humans takes a relentless and crafty propaganda campaign. You cannot simply send out an email at the start of the project or have a dull speaker say a few lame remarks at the kick-off meeting. That is not enough. You need evangelical experts who can spread the gospel of the new system. And if it's a small project that we are talking about, then it's on you. You need to be the one to inspire the troops to embrace the coming changes.

To embrace change, you must first and foremost, embrace the art and practice of professional change management, and in doing so your organization will embrace change, and suddenly you will stand a chance of success. But obviously, change management alone will not suffice. You also need to know what needs to change. You will be surprised by the answer because it's not what you think.

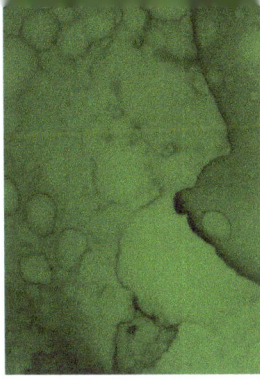

CHAPTER 1

Simplify Our Lives

A monk said to master Chao Chou,
"I have just entered the monastery for the first time.
Please teach me the Tao."

Chao Chou said, "Have you eaten the morning meal?"

The monastic said, "Yes, I have."

Chao Chou said, "Go wash your bowls."

Simplify Our Lives

We need to embrace change and the first thing that needs to change is our attitude and the attitudes of the entire organization. Change management is the answer. Change management is a field unto itself, and it is not the topic of this book. Learn about change management and hire change management consultants and make them an integral part of your IT project. Now that you and your entire organization are ready to embrace change, let's talk about what needs to change first. Surprisingly, it's not your IT system. There is first, a very important prerequisite. We must simplify our lives before we even begin to embark upon a major IT overhaul. Simplification, not sophistication or complication, is the hallmark of effectiveness and prosperity.

This Core Concept Component, Simplify Our Lives, comes first, because it is the most often neglected, and yet, it is the most important. IT projects are undertaken to replace outdated, unsupported, un-automated, non-integrated, antique systems. Everyone inside and outside the organization is well aware, from the janitors to the C-Levels, that the system is ludicrously out-of-date and inefficient. The idea is to replace the existing system with a brand spanking new modern system that will solve all the problems of the crappy old system. Traditionally, the first step is for business analysts (who may be internal to your organization or external consultants) to document the "as is" current state business processes and then provide a list of IT systems requirements.

This is the exact moment where everything goes horribly wrong.

The first step should NOT be to study the current state as a source of requirements. The current state is bad. The current state contains business rules, policies, and strategies that nobody has questioned or even looked at for decades! Yes, the current software system is inefficient, but that is just part of the problem, and believe it or not, it is not the biggest part. The biggest problem is that the policies of the organization are creating unnecessary complexity and busy work. Why is this the case? Everybody in the organization from the corporate officers to the divisional managers, to the supervisors, to the workers in the field are at all times busy keeping up with customer orders and/or trying to sell more services or products to expand the business. Nobody, and I mean, nobody, ever takes the time to question any of the business rules, policies, or strategies of the organization. What happens is that a new software package is selected and then licensed, and a consulting firm is engaged to implement the new software, and those consultants strive to configure the new software to process the functions demanded by the unquestioned policies that are needlessly causing all the extra complexity that leads to the so-called "requirements" being such a heavy lift. The "requirements" are not true requirements. The "requirements" are the sickening side-effects of toxic organizational policies!

There are two possibilities for what happens next. Either the entire project fails because the new software is unable to be configured in the allotted time to handle the needless complexity of the unquestioned organizational policies which make the requirements so difficult, or the implementation consultants are able to stand up the new system, which is actually a worse result, in a way, because the result is that you end up using new good software to perpetuate and cement in old bad policies.

It is true that the newer software will be better simply because it runs on the latest operating system, has more features, more and better reporting capabilities, and has a more open and robust application programming interface (API) meaning it can interface more easily to other applications and outside parties such as suppliers, government agencies, couriers, and banks. In most cases, the new software will also be an improvement, because unlike the legacy system, it is fully supported by the software developer, whereas the legacy system is often woefully behind in upgrades and has reached a point of being un-upgradeable. In fact, in many cases, the original software developer has long since gone out of business, and the system is being supported by a geriatric ex-employee of the developer who is brought out of retirement for side-work and dials in sporadically from a retirement community in Florida.

However, new software is not enough. Yes, you want the most current versions of widely adopted apps and the new cloud-based software-as-a-service (SaaS) subscription model puts you on apps that are continuously and automatically upgraded by the software developer which is a good thing. But unless you first clean house on your organizational policies with the beneficial result of simplifying your life, you will just be wasting your time and money by putting in a new system that serves the policies of your old dysfunctional world.

People feel they can skip this step because they mistakenly believe that the IT consultants whom they hired to implement their new software system will not only stand up the new system, but in the process of analysis and solutioning, they will keep an eye out for efficiency gains. The consultants repeat the mantra of "let's not just keep doing it the old way, because that's how we always did it, let's think outside the box, and come up with a new process." Everybody gets a warm fuzzy feeling that they are really going to make positive changes, and not just slap in new software which repeats the sins of the past, but they are mistaken.

The problem is that most IT projects lack budgeted hours for a comprehensive and far-reaching organizational policy review, and the application specialists that are configuring your software aren't industry-specific management consultants but are typically just folks that know where the setup screens are in one particular application or module of an application. What is needed is a bright spotlight shined into the heart of the what, why and wherefores of your organizational machine.

Functional application consultants who are on tight deadlines and operating under tight budget constraints are concerned primarily with getting you up and running on the new software as soon as possible, not with questioning your policies at any kind of deep and underlying level. Furthermore, they are typically not given any access to the people at your organization that could approve or enforce a major policy change. They never even talk to those folks; instead, they are tied up in meetings with end-users and figuring out how to configure the new software to perpetuate the old inefficient and unexamined policies.

Policy changes need to be approved and sanctioned by the appropriate authorities which could include the CEO, COO, CIO, CTO, CFO, Vice President of Sales, Vice President of Marketing, Director of Human Resources, Divisional Directors, Branch Managers, Board of Directors, and other leaders in your organization. It is not okay to simply say these people are all too busy and they will not have any bandwidth to look at any of these policies, and then just give up. Yes, the truth is that they are all always too busy. The CEO may be on the sales side or the product side, but they are always swamped. The COO is busy with day-to-day operations and is putting out fires. The VP of Sales is about to close a major deal. The CFO is either tied up in trying to close the books and issue financial statements or perhaps raising money in the form of private equity or bank loans. If the CFO can't raise the capital the whole business goes under. Nobody has any time. Their time is already fully booked in keeping up with the day-to-day demands of running the organization. They are in a battle for survival.

The fact that everybody who is in charge of making, approving, and enforcing policies is too busy to do any of that means you either need to hire new internal resources who will not be assigned to any day-to-day demands, and/or you need to hire a consulting firm that can provide management consultants. Management consultants are industry experts who know your type of business and have seen other similar businesses or organizations and will study your policies and compare them to industry best practices. They can act as an outside unbiased third-party that scrutinizes what you are doing and compares your policies and strategies to peers in your industry or organizational sector and advises you on how to clean up your act and streamline and simplify the way you operate.

It is truly amazing how this first and most important step is almost always entirely missing from the IT roadmap and the IT project plan. We cannot emphasize this enough.

SIMPLIFY YOUR POLICIES **BEFORE** you even think about embarking on any kind of major IT systems overhaul. People rarely do this, but this is the first and most important step. What a shame. This is one of the main reasons IT projects fail. If you want to succeed, you cannot afford to neglect this step. Please embrace this wisdom. Simplify our lives.

There is a terrible ignorance at the root of this problem which is this: complexity is not free just because you don't bother to notice or measure it. Here is the textbook example of the problem. Your marketing department is tasked with increasing your sales. Your marketing experts devise an ingenious customer discount policy which works to entice customers to make more purchases. Your thinking is that the increase in sales volume makes up for the lower price you are charging your customer; hence you think that you created a positive net income gain on your bottom line. But unfortunately, you have created yet another money pit. You never bothered to measure the administrative and IT cost of maintaining that overly complex discount policy. The policy is so complicated that your accounting department ended up hiring (unbeknownst to you) an outside programmer to code a special workaround to trick your ERP system into swapping out the normal price that comes up on the order screen. When you combine the cost of the custom programming and all the headaches caused by this complication which caused the billing manager to hire an extra employee in the accounting department as well, you are now operating at a net loss if you measure the gain from the new sales that were caused by the enticement of the discount scheme against the extra IT and administrative cost.

Furthermore, because not everything can be measured in dollars and cents you may not be sure whether the discount policy is helping or hurting; this is typical; you cannot even gauge whether your policies are a boost or detriment to your bottom line. Many people have the mistaken idea that we can measure everything and put a monetary number on absolutely everything if we choose to do so. But that is not true at all. You cannot measure everything. Let's go back to our example above. You cannot ever know how many sales were made only as the result of the new complicated discount scheme. Some customers might have bought the stuff anyway. You don't know for sure. You can never know. The IT costs are buried in the IT budget and even if the IT costs are then allocated out to departments, cost centers, profit centers, or branch offices, allocations are always a rough estimate based upon some arbitrary rule involving headcounts or something that doesn't really tell the whole story.

This is where you simply need to use common sense. As a general rule, eliminate any complicated schemes unless it is completely and overwhelmingly obvious that the complexity is unavoidable or that the complexity is really having an immense and overwhelming positive financial or otherwise beneficial outcome. What we have seen time and time again, is tons of complexity for complexity's sake, without any regard for the downstream IT and admin cost. It's just sad. Just plain sad. Let's get happy. Simply your life!

What kind of "policies" are we talking about here?

There may be many impactful policies that are unique to your industry or organizational sector or even unique to your particular organization; however, that being said, we see the same trouble spots appear again and again across a broad range of industries. Below is a list of policies to examine. If you don't have time to do it yourself (and you won't), then hire experts to do it for you, and then please go one step further and do the unthinkable, actually take the advice of the experts that you handsomely paid for and change your needlessly complex policies!

Opportunities to Simplify Your Life

- Doing Business in Unprofitable States, Provinces, or Countries
- Compliance with Highly Demanding States, Provinces, or Countries
- Tax Schemes that Require Splintered Incorporated Entities
- Outsourcing or Not Outsourcing
- Sales Commissions and Bonus Plans
- Customer Discount Schemes
- Document Printing and Storage Habits
- Customer and Vendor Rebate Schemes
- Inventory Valuation Methods
- Fixed Assets Capitalization Thresholds
- Tiny Revenue Streams and One-off Special Jobs and Projects
- Useless and Ignored Managerial Reports (that you keep on running)
- Overly Exacting Allocations and Accruals
- The list is endless…

We cannot talk at length about all of these opportunities to simplify our lives because they are too numerous to mention. We are drowning in a vast ocean of needless complexity. Nonetheless, we would be remiss if we failed to explain a few of the items on the list above in a bit more detail.

Here is a typical example of doing business in unprofitable areas. You open a small branch office in California which represents only 2% of your company's revenue and it's losing money anyway. California has very demanding compliance requirements and very complex tax jurisdictions and these cannot be ignored because you are doing business in California and the penalties for non-compliance are harsh. What happens next is your IT department is called in to deal with the new "requirements" for your ERP system and your custom reporting. You then embark upon a very expensive IT project which ultimately costs you more than the entire revenue generated by the California office (which is actually operating at a loss anyway). The misunderstanding here is that people think you need to add the California compliance functionality to the California TRANSACTIONS in your IT system, but that it wrong. You need to add the California compliance functionality to the ENTIRE IT system! Therefore, the entire IT system is modified to deal with a handful of unprofitable transactions. What a waste of time, effort, and money!

For your IT system to handle difficult transactions you must add the complex additional functionality to your ENTIRE system! This problem occurs for unprofitable customers, order types, difficult regions, persnickety counties, states, provinces, countries, customers, job types, service types, product types, and on and on. Unless you are really going to make an overwhelming amount of additional profit, it is not worth the trouble to do business in areas that cause additional complexity to your IT system or to add new products or services (new lines of business) that will have low volume but require extensive additional complexity demands to your IT systems.

It is truly flabbergasting how nobody seems to get this. Everybody is blinded by the glitter and glamour of new markets and more revenue. But that approach is foolish. You must factor in the added IT and administrative costs, and really try to understand what those costs are likely to realistically be, before venturing into new territories, launching new lines of business, or enacting new policies, schemes, or business rules.

People know that IT, administrative, bookkeeping, and accounting services are neither free nor readily plentiful; however, because they don't see the IT costs and clerical bookkeeping costs getting allocated to those specific difficult transactions, but rather just lumped in to a general and administrative bucket (called G&A costs), and then perhaps roughly allocated out to cost centers, they cannot see how harmful those specific nasty little useless transactions are to their bottom line. Sadly, in three decades time, we have never seen a study conducted at any enterprise to root out troublesome low volume transactions which are causing excessive IT and admin burdens. Instead, the troublesome transactions are heralded and applauded as inroads into new markets. They are not inroads into new markets. They are a dangerous money drain in most cases. You are much better off "sticking to the knitting" as they say. Make money by focusing on profitable transactions in areas and of types that do not demand excessive complexity and compliance demands. Obviously, we are not saying that you shouldn't do business in California, which is a world economic superpower unto itself and an important agriculture and technology center. We are just saying that you need to consider the IT and administrative costs of rouge outlier transactions that demand complex changes to your IT system or complex so-called requirements.

Another sacrosanct policy that needs to be questioned is breaking up a single company into multiple entities incorporated in different states or provinces for the purpose of tax advantages. The savings in taxes are unfortunately not compared with the extra cost involved in developing and maintaining an IT system that must cope with the artificial splintering of the unified company into dozens of separated business or organizational entities each with their own tax ID number and separate set of books. Intercompany transactions and due to / due from accounting is the inevitable result. Shared master files and chart of accounts get out of sync. Financial statements and management reporting is made much more complex. The IT cost of these added complexities may actually exceed the original tax savings. Often times the tax savings were fleeting as tax authorities rip away corporate veils and close up loopholes. As the tax savings disappear, there is no longer a reason for the companies to be split out into dozens of pieces; however, the entrenched IT system is unable to be easily or quickly adapted to account for a consolidated entity. The needless fracture of the business entity into artificial pieces often persists for years. At the start of a new major IT project, the possibility of consolidating entities that are needlessly splintered should be a key goal.

Payroll and Human Resources can be and often should be outsourced. The enormous complexity of administering employee compensation and benefits plans is increasing as new laws, regulations, and guidelines arise continuously. Reporting to taxing authorities is a job unto itself. For example, we know of a company that wanted help selecting a new ERP package to replace a sunset product (a software package which the developer is no longer improving and is encouraging their customers to migrate away from). This company insisted on running their own payroll internally. The ERP software selection, therefore, included the "requirement" that the software must include a robust payroll module; however, few ERP software offerings these days include payroll functionality because nowadays most companies outsource the payroll function to ADP, Ceridian, Paychex, UKG, Insperity, and other payroll and benefits outsourcers. What happened is that the software selection was erroneously constrained to a very limited list of potential products. They ended up selecting a software that is not widely adopted in their industry nor their country with the hopes that it would become more widely adopted in the future, but that didn't happen. All of this came about because the first step was finding software to fulfill a so-called requirement. The first step needs to be questioning the so-called requirements by conducting an up-front policy study and having the wisdom and the courage to embrace change and do away with entrenched yet illogical policies (in this case, the policy was that we must run our own payroll internally instead of outsourcing it). It was illogical for that company to process their own payroll when they could have easily outsourced it as most companies do, and as a result of being too afraid and narrow minded to change their old policy, they artificially limited their choice of a new ERP system which had detrimental results on several levels.

Sales commission and employee bonus plans are a notorious area for needless complexity. We know of a case where a company invented a load factor which was an arbitrary percentage that decreased the gross profit margin on sales thereby lowering the commission payable to the sales rep, because the commission was calculated as a commission percentage multiplied by the gross profit amount. By reducing the gross profit amount by applying the "load factor", they reduced the commission amount to be paid to the rep. Of course, they could have simply lowered the sales rep's commission percentage. This is a perfect example of needless complexity. We have a sales amount minus the cost amount which equals the gross profit amount. We multiply the gross profit amount by, for example, 5% as the commission rate and we get the amount to pay the sales rep for his or her commission for that sale. That is simple.

But unfortunately, they introduced another variable, the load factor. Why? Because they can then pay the sales rep less than 5% and still claim to be giving them a 5% commission rate. These psychological head games are often the culprit behind the evolution of commission schemes that end up as hideously complex Rube Goldberg machines. More and more variables and nuances are introduced into the scheme to keep all the players happy so that nobody feels they are getting ripped off. This kind of nonsense goes on all the time and the IT cost to handle the needless complexity is neither measured nor questioned.

We know of another firm that devised a bonus plan that was so complicated that the explanation of the calculation was a 150-page PDF file (that nobody had time to read, of course). In the end, the firm declined to pay any bonus due to an economic downturn and the plan was scrapped; however, the firm did pay for the resources to devise the scheme, document the scheme in a 150-page memorandum, and perform the calculation throughout the year, and make the necessary IT changes to the accounting software to accommodate the new plan. The cost of devising and maintaining the plan was more than whatever morale boost it was supposed to provide (and yet failed to yield).

Why not just pay everybody a flat percentage of their salary plus a discretionary flat amount decided on by the manager which is not to exceed some reasonable percentage of their salary? Such a common-sense bonus plan can be explained in a simple email and calculated and maintained easily. Why do people create needless complexity? Why play these stupid head games? We can simplify our lives, and we MUST simplify our lives BEFORE we can successfully revamp our IT systems.

What to expense versus what to capitalize? What to measure individually versus what to lump together? What to track versus what to not worry about? These are important policy questions. They are prerequisites to IT system requirements; they are not IT system questions. These policy questions must be studied, simplified, and acted upon PRIOR TO any major IT systems revamping project. For example, as a general rule of thumb, expense small items. The IT and admin cost of tracking individual screws, tacks, and paperclips exceeds the cost of those items. Why are you tracking it then?

The KISS principle (Keep It Simple Stupid) should be your guiding light in the all-important prerequisite endeavor to simplify our lives by changing organizational policies that spawn needless complexity. In discussing some of the typical organizational policies that entail needless complexity, we considered the IT and administrative cost of upholding those policies. Don't stop there. Go even further and consider other costs as well such as transportation, sales tax, rent, office supplies, repair and maintenance, utilities, telecommunications, network and cloud storage, and vendor services of all kinds; these are typical examples of the hidden costs of unexamined illogical organizational policies.

A good example is storing paper. Why create the paperwork in the first place. Contact a paperless workflow automation specialist and let them show you their cost studies which include hidden costs such as increased office rent due to physical file cabinets taking up more and more square footage in your offices.

And not only do you need to get rid of bad policies BEFORE your next IT systems overhaul, but you also need to get rid of bad data BEFORE as a PREREQUISITE to beginning an IT system revamping. Bad data is usually considered to be a mere afterthought and the time and money spent cleaning up your data, such as your list of vendors, customers, contacts, inventory items, product codes, warehouses, facilities, and branch office locations, and so forth, is buried within the IT systems implementation task typically described as data conversion or data migration. In a project plan for a new ERP implementation, for instance, there are a certain number of estimated hours budgeted for the data migration. The data will be extracted from the old system and cleaned up in Excel, then imported into the new system using Excel templates, or better yet SQL stored procedures will be developed to query the legacy data and automatically transform it into records that can be imported into the new system.

Implementing a new IT system is not the time to clean up your lousy data, because by taking that approach, you are adding a difficult and risky project with an unpredictable timeframe (namely, the data clean-up project) to an even more risky project with a tight timeframe (namely, the IT system implementation project). You need to assess how bad your data is ahead of time, and then clean it up in the old system. Then when you start implementing the new system, you will still have a challenge to extract the old data (which at least has been cleaned up ahead of time) and transform it into records which will be compatible with the new software. Data transformation is enough of a challenge, but to combine that challenge with the challenge of data cleansing is asking for trouble. Have the discipline and the forethought to embark upon data cleanups BEFORE you even think about changing your IT systems. For example, what is stopping you right now from inactivating duplicate customers or vendors in the legacy system, ahead of time? Why does this have to wait until you are officially hot and heavy into implementing a new IT system? The answer is that it doesn't it. It's an excuse. You are just kicking the can down the road. You are putting off cleaning up your room until guests arrive for the holiday visit. That is wrong. Clean up your room now!

It's a real no-brainer. We can save so much money by using computer technology. However, if your IT projects keep failing and being scrapped, not only do you suffer the loss of the money you spent on the IT project itself which is just money down the drain, but you also suffer the opportunity cost of the years lost where you could have been reaping the rewards of the new technology in the form of substantial annual savings. You need to learn these Core Concept Components to ensure that your IT projects will succeed. Please read on.

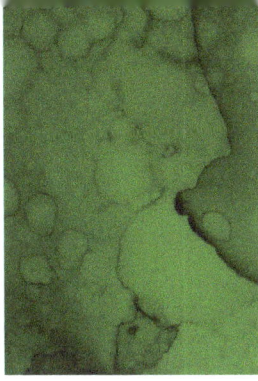

CHAPTER 2

Enrich Us All

In spring, hundreds of flowers; in autumn, a harvest moon;

In summer, a refreshing breeze; in winter, snow accompanies you.

When useless things do not hang in the mind,

Every season is your best season.

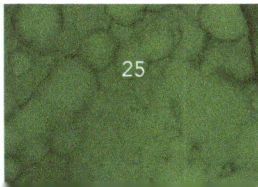

Enrich Us All

Information technology is powerful and should be used to enrich us all. As your not-for-profit organization reduces costs due to computer automation your workers are able to provide more and better services to the community. As your business leverages automated, integrated, cloud-based applications, profits increase, enriching shareholders as well as employees who participate in compensation plans tied to profits, who may own stock, and who can get wage increases which the company can now afford to pay the workers. It is a win-win situation.

If we ask the question: why are we even bothering to try to improve or replace an IT system? The answer is obvious. It is because we want to be more profitable, and in the case of a not-for-profit institution, we want to have the wherewithal to provide more charitable services. The bottom line is, well, for lack of a better term, THE BOTTOM LINE. We must ask this question, first and foremost: what is the benefit of investing in this endeavor? To this end, management at many organizations requires that a return on investment (ROI) study be prepared to justify any IT spend. However, ROI is not a perfect concept. ROI is impossible to compute accurately due to intangible factors. Every ROI study must boil down to a currency amount. The cost of doing it versus the cost of not doing it. The ROI study computes whether doing it pays over some period of time, usually about five years. If the ROI is a positive amount, then the project is green lighted, if it is a negative amount, then the project's funding is denied.

The textbook ROI example goes something like this; a company can opt to buy a new machine for their factory to replace the existing machine. The new machine costs $100,000. However, the new machine uses only half the electricity because it runs more efficiently. The cost of electricity for the old machine is at least $200,000 per year. Therefore, within one year the company will save enough money on reduced electricity costs to pay for the new machine. Every year thereafter, they will be saving an additional $100,000. Other cost-saving factors can be added in such as the lower cost of maintenance of the new machine. The old machine required a guy named Juan who was the only chap that knew how to keep the old dinosaur relic of a machine operational. By purchasing the new machine, we can send Juan to an early retirement; we can factor in eliminating Juan's salary, benefits, and other carrying costs as additional savings.

ROI is a really good thing and of course, you should always try to do it. But you must keep in mind that reality is infinitely complex, and ROI is a mere model of reality. All sorts of additional intangible factors will inevitably come into play in all situations. That is why you need to use good old-fashioned common sense and you also need to follow your gut instincts. To return to the example of Juan. It turns out that Juan was such a popular chap at the company that getting rid of him caused an avalanche of departures. Juan was hired by a rival firm, and he started to tell folks about how much better this other company was to its employees. The heavy turnover resulted in massive recruiting and temporary employee fees charged by staffing agencies. Furthermore, the new machine produced a slightly inferior product, and the assumption was that customers wouldn't notice, but they did notice, and they left in droves. The decision to buy the new machine was a disaster. You cannot reduce reality to numerical figures on a spreadsheet.

Now let's turn to a real-world example of how absurd it can get. We know of a large and successful wholly owned subsidiary of a Fortune 500 company that needed to upgrade their ERP system because it had not been upgraded in almost ten years and the version they were running was no longer supported by Microsoft. The parent company, as part of their IT policy, insisted that all IT projects must have a positive ROI. You needed to show how spending money on the IT project would result in more profits. There was no way to calculate in a neat little formula (or even a complex formula) how upgrading the ERP would result in more profits or cost savings and certainly no way to provide a precise dollar amount or even a ballpark estimate amount. In fact, upgrading the ERP was going to be costly and would not result in an uptick in sales or a reduction of operational costs. But the fact remained that they were running a multi-million-dollar subsidiary on an unsupported ERP package. At moments like this, common sense should take over the conversation. The upgrade project OBVIOUSLY needed to be approved because OBVIOUSLY it would be wrong to allow the subsidiary to continue to run all their mission critical accounting, billing, inventory, field services, and trade and logistics functions on an unsupported software and an unsupported operating system. Happily, common sense did prevail, and the IT project was approved and was successful.

Brace yourself for a shocking but true statement. Calculating ROI is a good practice in general but calculating the ROI of improving your IT systems is a waste of time. It's an obvious fact that if you don't keep up with the advances in computer technology you will fall behind and the competition will eat you alive. You must improve and modernize your IT systems. We have seen too many outdated processes such as receiving faxes that get printed out, then stamped with a rubber stamp, then annotated with a magic marker, then scanned at a copier, then browsed to on a network folder in Windows Explorer, then copied to another network folder, then renamed, then printed to a PDF printer which creates a PDF file, then renamed yet again, then attached to an email, then detached by the email recipient who renames the file yet again and uploads it to SharePoint, where it gets downloaded by some other employee, who prints the damn thing out, brings it to his desk and types the data into an Excel spreadsheet that is stored on Dropbox! We have seen the madness. Why are these kinds of dreadfully inefficient and illogical workflows still so prevalent in organizations to this day?

The illogical data dances are still going on because your IT projects keep failing or worse yet, you are too traumatized, scared, and bitter to start up a new major IT overhaul. But you must not give up. You must not lose hope. If you absorb the nine Core Concept Components of the Zen of IT, your IT projects will succeed, and everyone involved will reap enormous rewards. You need to improve your terribly inefficient IT systems. That can't happen unless your IT projects succeed. Too many of your IT projects end in failure and the end-users end up trapped on the old systems for many years into the future. We know this is happening all over the world. How can we stop it?

As we learned in the previous chapter, first, we need to simplify our lives by questioning our organizational policies and in doing so weed out needless complexity; this will drastically reduce the difficulty of the IT system requirements, giving you a chance to succeed. But this is just step one. In step one we targeted illogical policies that lead to bogus "requirements" which result in wasteful IT and admin spending.

Overkill Functionality

Now in step two we target overkill IT functionality that provides useless capabilities which results in wasteful IT spending, and worse yet can sink a project in the same way bad organizational policies can. Information technology is a great thing, but you don't need a sledgehammer to kill a mosquito. IT consulting firms and software developers sell flyswatters as well as sledgehammers. They like to sell sledgehammers because they make more money that way. A big part of making sure that you don't lose sight of the bottom line is to avoid making the mistake of information technology for information technology's sake. Just as complexity for complexity's sake is a mistake, worshipping computer technology as an answer for everything that ails you is a grave error. Computers are great and they should be used wisely to target areas where processes can be automated and integrated, and pertinent accurate information made easily and widely available to all authorized parties inside and outside your organization who need that information.

However, unfortunately, many people who plan IT projects get dazzled by the technological possibilities and they lose sight of the bottom line.

The main progenitor of IT overkill is the idea that you need to measure and report on every miniscule meaningless detail of your operations because you believe that information is like money, the more the better. The idea that we can and should measure, track and report on absolutely everything under the sun is erroneous and dangerous. This is business stupidity not business intelligence. Time and time again we have seen well-meaning managers demand that IT systems are enhanced to track all kinds of tiny little meaningless items creating a Rubik's cube reporting system of bewildering proportions. That manager may enjoy solving a Rubik's cube as a challenging game that makes their job more interesting, but it does nothing for the bottom line of their organization. IT solution providers encourage this kind of thinking because they want to sell you the reporting software and charge you for the services to develop, maintain and enhance it.

Imagine a pizzeria. The pizzeria has three employees. Tony makes the pizza. His sister Angie works the register, and the old man, Luigi, sweeps up and works in the back. This business is descended upon by a hoard of well-meaning consultants and managers who have MBAs from prestigious universities. They devise an IT system that will measure exactly how many revolutions Tony makes when he spins a pizza dough and in which direction, and it takes into account the air temperature and barometric pressure. They are trying to make the business more efficient by knowing everything about the operations. The problem is that now Tony needs to remember how many spins each pizza dough gets, and he has to stop what he is doing to take meteorological readings and then key the information into a laptop. Meanwhile Angie has to take one hour to explain to each customer the wonderful new discount policy devised by the marketing MBA which gives a multi-tiered graduated discount percentage based upon the day of the week, the time of day, and amount of pepperoni, and the whether or not you have purchased before, whether you have a customer rewards card, whether the card is the bronze, silver, or gold level or super special VIP level, and whether you are considered a senior, a student, or a preferred customer. Within a few months the pizzeria, which had been operating at a profit for more than fifty years, goes out of business.

The pizzeria example only seems ridiculous because it is a tiny little business; however, this kind of needless reporting complexity thrives in larger organizations, and it is rarely questioned. The problem is that managers are hired to improve the organization and they need to justify their existence, so they become ravenous for information because they believe it will make them seem like they are sophisticated geniuses that deserve to be earning their generous salary. These same managers should instead participate in studies designed to streamline their organizational policies to weed out and eradicate needless complexity, and to make the organization more efficient and therefore more effective and profitable through drastically reducing wasteful general and administrative operating expenses, instead of adding yet more needless complexity.

IT overkill isn't confined to reporting requirements but that is where it usually rears its ugly head. However, overblown reporting requirements can easily derail your IT project, so eliminate them. Most information becomes random noise if you drill down too far into the weeds. To return to the example of Tony in the pizzeria. Useful information would be how many pizzas does he make each day that go unsold and roughly speaking what is the cost of the material and labor to make those pizzas. That information could be used to determine that he is making too many pizzas ahead of time. However, information junkies go too far. They become obsessive about drilling into every detail, and they want to know precisely how many flakes of oregano are on each slice of pizza. Again, this example seems silly, but it illustrates a major IT problem that is widespread.

Everyone assumes that all information is good. Information is understood to be a universal good such as Love, Peace, or Health. It is not. So-called information is mostly useless noise. The cost of hiring IT professionals to create databases, OLAP cubes, data warehouses, big data repositories, reporting data marts, refreshable Excel pivot tables, SQL queries, Tableau and Power BI dashboards, and artificial intelligence algorithms to report on all this meaningless noise is substantial and wasteful and it derails IT projects. Whether the crazy reporting requirements needlessly increase the cost of your IT project or in fact, actually sink the entire project will be unknown. In either case, these kinds of overreaching reporting requirements are a major factor in why IT projects cost too much, take too long, and often fail.

Instead of focusing on information, and instead of insisting on having every little tiny bit of information, and instead of trying to quantify each tiny little fraction of it, you should instead use your common sense and settle on reasonable IT system requirements. The erroneous idea that a new IT system must deliver every bit of information about your entire operations along with a precise financial numeric value is a project killer. You cannot measure everything. You cannot know everything. And here is the wonderful and glorious secret: you don't need to. You can enrich us all, by being reasonable, rational, level-headed, and logical. Reduce your IT requirements. Reduce your overblown information requirements as well. These are your first two steps toward IT project success.

Materiality is an accounting term which means that accuracy is not required if the financial impact of the inaccuracy is below a percentage threshold. For example, if your bank reconciliation is off by two cents and your bank balance is ten million dollars and your bank transactions that month are ten thousand transactions with deposits and withdrawals exceeding one hundred million dollars, the auditors will in all likelihood let you slide on the two cents. Accountants are smart enough to adhere to the materiality principle and it is in their DNA to do so. However, in the IT world, materiality is too often overlooked when gauging the validity and necessity of a so-called IT systems requirement.

A real-world example of this that we came across was an IT project that spanned six months and required a full-time SQL programmer working forty hours per week. The project was an enhancement to a payroll system that enabled payroll to be processed in Guam which is a U.S. Island territory located in Micronesia. Sadly, nobody involved in the planning or approving of the project bothered to ask what percentage of the employees worked in Guam. As it turned out, there was one employee in Guam who worked there for three weeks, out of a total of over 15,000 employees who were employed during that same year. You may wonder how something that ridiculous could be allowed to happen, but this kind of thing is the norm in the IT world. Here is how it happens. A staffing recruiter received a phone call from somebody in Guam, and not wanting to lose any opportunity to add more staffing placements, he arranged for the work to be conducted. The payroll and human resources team in the course of doing their jobs realized that the Guam location would not be accommodated by their current IT process. They then requested that the IT department accommodate the requirement.

Clearly there should be a review process in which proposed IT projects are rejected if the functionality requested by the business is needed only in a few rare cases. It is amazing how much of this kind of ridiculous programming slips through the cracks and gets approved or just happens as well-meaning people-pleasing coders and project managers endeavor to make the end-users happy. When gathering requirements for your next big IT project, you must remember Guam. How many of your so-called requirements are akin to the lonely soul on the island of Guam who quit after three weeks. You should not approve or include tricky and difficult programming, application enhancements, and special reporting that will take money, time, and substantial effort, and entail risk when the functionality addresses rare oddball one-offs that should be handled outside the system and estimated to your best ability.

But we have found that the philosophy of rejecting immaterial requirements is too often not followed, especially when scoping out major IT overhauls or complete system replacements. Too often all requirements, even if they relate to one customer, one vendor, one employee, one type of product, one jurisdiction, one locality, one sales rep, one office, one rebate policy, or one pricing nuance, are considered real, valid, and important requirements. Why? Because they are real customers, vendors, employees, products, and so forth. In other words, the transaction is something that really happened. There is a real honest-to-goodness transaction that occurred under the bizarre and rare scenario. Therefore, the erroneous thinking is that it is a real requirement because it is part of reality. While it is part of reality, it should be handled outside the IT system proper, most likely using an Excel worksheet and in all likelihood a somewhat inaccurate guesstimate will suffice to satisfy the auditors due to the immaterial nature of the event.

The first two Core Concept Components, **Simplify Our Lives** and **Enrich Us All** are closely related. Both of these Core Concept Components are about reducing requirements. One would think that the idea of reducing requirements is obvious, but as you should be able to see by now, it is not. In IT parlance we talk about scope creep. Scope creep is where the requirements creep up as the users ask for more and more features in the midst of the design phase. Scope creep is a problem but do not confuse these Core Concept Components with mere scope creep. We are talking about something much more insidious and overreaching and we are enlightening you with wisdom which is much more profound. You must understand that the requirements are problematic not only when they creep upward during design, but even way before you begin to plan your IT project because the requirements are rotten at their core. Then even after you have had the courage and wisdom to simplify our lives by simplifying your organizational policies, you still need to question your gluttony for information and your people-pleasing obsession with handling every kind of transaction within the new system.

IT, as you know, stands for Information Technology. Information is worshipped like a God. But information is not God, and it's not even good. Information is mostly noise because you can keep on drilling into it forever until you reach level after level of random chaotic dissonance. Even though Dr. Mandelbrot showed us that there are patterns in chaos which can be geometrically understood, we don't need to delve into that level of complexity for the purposes of running a typical business enterprise or a not-for-profit organization. Furthermore, a precise currency amount cannot be accurately assigned to every little bit of miniscule information. Information is too often thought to be immediately and easily translated into numeric financial figures that can then be put through a formula that then tells you what to do. This is nonsense. Most of what transpires in reality is intangible. Our computerized recorded transactions are crude models of reality that are assigned estimated numerical values for the purpose of facilitating trade. Reality is analog. Reality cannot be atomized, quantified, and numerically valued in its totality. You must arbitrarily select a reasonable level of detail and adopt a reasonable, simple, and elegant model. That model will be useful, but it will not accurately represent the infinite nature of reality.

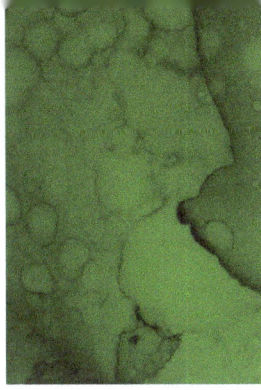

CHAPTER 3

Empower Our Future

A monk asked the Master:
"Can you help me understand my past lives?
Can you help me understand my future lives?"

The Master said, "If you wish to understand your past lives,
look at your present life. If you wish to understand your
future lives, look at your present life."

Empower Our Future

Embracing change requires inspiring our people to adopt new technology to do their jobs more efficiently; professional change management expertise can help us accomplish this. Change management must be taken seriously and be an integral part of your next IT project. Furthermore, as you learned with the last two Core Concept Components, you must reduce your IT systems requirements before you even begin planning your IT project, as a prerequisite, by first examining your organizational policies and shedding needlessly complex processes, and by including only those transactional scenarios that are both profitable and material in nature, and by cleaning up your master data records directly in the legacy system, not putting it off until the data migration phase of the new system implementation.

Much of the wisdom shared in these pages is concerned with what to do before you embark on your digital transformation journey. If you start the journey unprepared, then it's already too late. You have already failed. You don't need to wait the full sixteen months, for example, until your IT project is scrapped, and you've flushed a million dollars down the toilet. You might as well not do the project, because the truth is that your IT project has failed before you even created a project plan. Embracing Change is about what you must do before you even consider embarking on a major IT revamping project, and this Core Concept Component, called **Empower Our Future**, teaches us about the attitude and the stance you must take before you announce the project or formulate a project charter and project plan.

With the third Core Concept Component, we Empower Our Future, by identifying and engaging the people in our organization who truly have the authority to enforce policy change and data clean up, as prerequisites, and who will continue to use their authority to enforce the adoption of the new IT system. Change management activities are aimed at priming the IT end-users for change, by fostering hope and confidence and dispelling fear and doubt. The change management activities soften the end-users up, butter them up, and help to make them somewhat more cooperative, less skeptical, and yes, less hostile. But that is about all change management can do. Change management cannot force the end-users to change their habits and adopt the new system. Change management can only make the users easier to deal with, and more likely to accept change less begrudgingly. It is up to the bosses to force the users to change, by making it crystal clear to them that the change is not optional. The boss has to tell the workers, "Either adopt the new system, or go work somewhere else, because using the new system is requirement of your employment". This has to be communicated clearly and under no uncertain terms.

However, a major reason why IT projects fail is because the managers are too weak, tepid, scared, or downright lily-livered to use their power to FORCE the end-users to adopt the new system. Also, many managers themselves do not want change. Furthermore, sometimes the managers are end-users themselves because they started in the business many years ago and they have a hard time letting go and delegating the system use to underlings as they themselves have advanced to higher levels of management. In those cases, the lines get very blurry, indeed; the high-level manager is an end-user and acts like an end-user (wanting the new system to duplicate the old system for instance). Another common scenario is for a manager, for example the Chief Financial Officer, to limit their involvement in the project so as to distance themselves from what they perceive to be an impending disaster. By staying uninvolved and uncommitted to the project's success, in their minds they avoid the risk of project failure, but in actuality, they are ensuring the project's failure with a self-fulfilling prophecy of doom. Their involvement is needed from a design perspective, from a morale perspective, and most importantly from an authority perspective.

Consider this. A worker might want more money. Who doesn't? But most people know that robbing a bank is not an option. Why? Because the police will arrest you and put you in prison, and they are serious about that. You cannot rob a bank, and then say you are sorry, and the judge will just let it slide. All it takes is one bank robbery and your life is forever altered. You will be found and arrested and the consequences are very severe. This is as it should be. Otherwise, we would have chaos. The same kind of stark simple brutal logic needs to be applied to multi-million-dollar IT projects. There is a lot of money at stake in a major IT system overhaul at a large organization. There is a lot at stake, relatively speaking, in a small or mid-sized business changing over their IT system as well. Many dozens, or hundreds, or even thousands of people are involved in the change which impacts everyone's job and affects everyone's livelihood. This is serious stuff, and it should be taken seriously. Robbing a bank is not an option. Rejecting the new IT system, likewise, must not be an option. If rejecting the new IT system is believed to be an option by the end-users, most of them will reject it. This is the stark reality that managers and business owners and IT consulting practice directors sometimes don't recognize.

What happens all too often at organizations embarking on IT system implementations is that the end-users of the IT system, get the idea that it is the job of the consultants to put in a new IT system, and they, the end-users are the customers, and the customer is king, and the customer is always right. To the end-users, getting a new ERP system is akin to having a new HVAC system installed in your home. It is the sole job of the HVAC technicians to install the new system and make it work. If the new system doesn't work to their satisfaction, they blame the HVAC company, and kick them out. They behave like consumers buying a product, a product that they can opt to reject and return to the store any time they want for a full refund if it doesn't measure up to their preferences and whims. This characterization might seem like an exaggeration, but it is not. We have seen this type of behavior over and over again.

Here is how this happens. The manager does not want the users to feel like they have little to no input, no choices, and no power in the process; therefore, the manager bends over backwards and over-compensates, and grants the users full veto power by making statements such as "if Jane isn't happy with the new billing system, then she doesn't have to use it." The user is empowered to reject the new system design by verbally stating something as simple as "it's not going to work for me" or "I'm not happy with it" or perhaps through a more formal sign-off process, by simply refusing to sign the design document, and making the system designer go back to the drawing board again and again until the system is reconfigured, customized, and modified to a point where it meet's Jane's satisfaction. The problem is that Jane will only be satisfied if the new system is overly customized to a point where it works the same way as the old outdated inefficient system we are replacing, because Jane's primary criterion for satisfaction is similarity to the legacy system which thereby allows her to avoid learning anything new. Again, this characterization sounds like a ridiculous exaggerated parody, but unfortunately this is often the reality. We have seen this type of dysfunctional end-user behavior over and over again. If management does not forcibly and overtly suppress this kind of behavior, then the consultants have no way to win, and everybody loses, as the IT project fails. The managers have wasted a great deal of organization's money, the IT consulting firm has lost a good reference and may in fact, be sued, and the end-users are still stuck on the old inefficient "dinosaur" system.

Often a failed IT project is perceived by the end-user to be a great relief; that's how bad it can get as far as dysfunctional attitudes, especially in projects without any effective change management expertise as an integral part of the project. The implementation consultants are IT big shots who are costing your organization a fortune in high hourly consulting fees, but yet despite that, they are often granted ZERO authority and ZERO power over any end-users. The IT consultants are outsiders, guests, temporary nuisances, not bosses. Unless the bosses of the end-users FORCE the end-users to refrain from bad behavior and wrong attitudes, with the threat of termination looming, the IT consultants are just sitting ducks, fish in a barrel, and easy prey for any end-user who simply does not want to adopt the new system for whatever reason. In the final analysis they will blame the software and blame the software consultants, then go back to double keying into their dumb terminal green screen application happily busying themselves with their tedious yet familiar and therefore comfortable non-automated process.

End-user bad behaviors and wrong attitudes come in a lot of flavors. None of this is malicious. The bad behavior and wrong attitudes stem from fear, ignorance, past trauma of previous failed IT projects, and the frailties of human nature. Examples of end-user bad behavior and wrong attitudes includes (but is not limited to) the following:

- Only happy if the new system works exactly like the old system as a strategy to avoid having to learn a new system.
- Finding fault with anything and everything as a strategy to derail or delay the adoption of the new system.
- Lack of active participation such as missing meetings, not reviewing design documents, and not bothering to log into the sandbox system to try it out.
- Lack of interest and overall apathy (attending meetings in body but daydreaming through them).
- Paranoia about the new system not handling certain types of rare and/or complex transactions or scenarios; always bringing up the rare scenario that proves why the new system won't work.
- Going off on tangents and getting lost in the weeds rather than dealing with the basic typical transaction first and foremost, and

then taking pride in how rigorous and thorough they are being, when in reality, they are ruining the project by making it impossible to come to agreement on basic design decisions.

- Neglecting to disclose vital requirements during the discovery and business analysis interviews and then suddenly remembering and injecting in major complex new requirements after a design had already been established, causing havoc with the project plan, and resulting in major rework as screens, reports, and/or workflows have to be scrapped and rebuilt to accommodate the newly revealed requirements.

We know of a case where a new financial statement for profit and loss (P&L) showing budget versus actual results for their branch offices was being developed as part of a new ERP implementation at a mid-market company. The programmer finished the report and presented it to the end-user. The end-user complained that the branch offices were not correctly sorted. The programmer then explained that the system works out-of-the-box in such a fashion as to sort the branch office by branch office number or description, and that the report sorts automatically by either office number or office description and was indeed working correctly, but that the old system was a hard-coded report that was actually sorting them incorrectly in a hard-coded manner that sorted by neither office number nor office description. The end-user then stated that neither the office number nor the office description would sort the report in the same sort order as the legacy version of the P&L, and that she would not sign off unless it worked just like the old system. The programmer then had to introduce a special customization which mis-sorted the offices to match the legacy sort. Now both the old report and the new report were identically mis-sorted. The extra programming took two weeks, cost thousands of dollars, and is just one tiny example of hundreds of similar illogical things that the IT consultants were forced to do because management allowed this kind of nonsense. The accumulated effect of all these extra customizations was enough to delay and eventually derail the project.

It might sound like we are coming down hard on the end-users, but the end-users are rarely to blame in IT project failure. Very often it's the IT folks that should be blamed for IT project failure. IT consultants as well as internal IT department managers are often the culprits in IT projects that go awry. We will get into those issues when we discuss the second Core Concept, **Seek Balance**.

Who is to blame? Who causes IT projects to fail?

It is typically not the end-users. ALMOST NEVER.

IT Project failure is Management failure!

It is almost always the Uppermost Top Management, the C-Levels, and other leadership roles as well such as Division Managers, Branch Managers, Vice Presidents, Human Resource Directors, and the Head of Project Management Office (PMO), and often because of believing in the exaggerated promises of IT salespeople and consultants who are quick to promise the sun, the moon, and the stars, underestimating the complexity and glossing over the details.

The end-users may engage in bad behavior and wrong attitudes, but only if their bosses let them do it. And their wrong attitude is often the result of their leadership not thinking they need to pay for change management expertise, and not hiring any change management consultants, and not doing any change management activities themselves to inspire the end-users to adopt positive attitudes. There are countless cases of major IT project initiatives being embarked upon where the CEO had nothing whatsoever to do with it, nothing to say about it, and remained completely uninvolved with it. There are cases where the accounting software was being replaced and the CFO was not involved and stayed out of the project completely, leaving it to the controller.

We know of one case where the COO wanted a completely new system for ERP, CRM, and HR, but the CEO of the same company did not want any changes and neither did the controller. They embarked upon the project hiring consultants and starting a project that they ran for about three years. After three years and a cost of well over a million dollars, they scrapped the project. This happened at a company with over 5,000 employees who were doing IT consulting work for blue chip clients. Their system was so non-automated and manually inefficient that the more than 5,000 employees at the company did not even have access to a timesheet entry application to key in their weekly timesheets. Instead, they filled out their timesheet in an Excel spreadsheet template and emailed the spreadsheet as an email attachment to the admin department. The time entry information was then hand-keyed into the NetSuite ERP Sales Order module. This was their non-automated and very inefficient method of billing which they could not improve even after three years of continuous and costly IT investments. The project was doomed to failure for a variety of reasons, but the main reason is that any major IT overhaul must have a unified front of solid and unflinching commitment from all the C-Level leadership. If the CEO, CFO, and COO are not unified in their desire and passion for digital transformation, then the project is doomed from the start.

The high-level management of your organization must step up and take a stand against end-user bad behavior and wrong attitudes. They must **Embrace Change** by embracing change management as a serious and necessary psychological component to IT system transformation success. They must talk about and cheerlead the IT project often, loudly, and passionately. The leaders of the company must make it clear to all employees that the change is not optional. The following are examples of the kind of statements that should be made by the organizational leadership on a regular basis in company meetings, on company memorandums, and as part of a well-orchestrated change management strategy:

- We're putting in a new system by next year at the latest, and everyone is required to learn it, use it, and do their utmost to adopt it.
- The new system is not going to be perfect, and it's up to you to work through the kinks during the first few months after go-live.
- We are giving out large bonuses to departments and branches that go live on the new system on schedule; if your branch is able to go live on time, then all employees in the branch get paid the bonus.
- If you expect to still have a job here in five years, we are going to have to put this new system in this year, because our competition has already adopted cloud-technology and has a fully automated ERP system.

In many instances, the top leadership at companies are too busy to bother much about IT projects. They are either tied up with legal, regulatory and compliance issues, putting out fires related to complaining customers, trying to expand into new markets, trying to raise capital, or trying to close on large deals. Sometimes they are more interested in office intrigue, battling each other with internal conflicts taking precedence over anything else. Sometimes they are simply absent, taking in the sunshine on a yacht floating in the Caribbean. They behave as though they are hiring a house painter to paint the powder room in their vacation home; their attitude is that the vendor will handle it.

When the top leadership thinks that they can hire an IT consulting firm to implement a new system for them and then hands that firm primary responsibility for getting the job done there is likely to be trouble. Sometimes top management may hire a few people internally as dedicated resources specifically placed on the project, but unfortunately, they tend to grant those folks very little authority over the end-users or operational directors, managers, and supervisors, and having no teeth, they are not listened to and prove to be very ineffective. And, as stated earlier, they most often embark on all of this without first examining and then simplifying their inefficient and needlessly complex business policies, without cleaning up their data in the legacy system, and without even a thought about change management.

Their flawed answer as to how to digitally transform their company by replacing the ERP, CRM, ECM, and HR systems (that may have been in place for multiple decades), is to budget about 20% of what it would realistically cost to do so, then hire a few new people (maybe a project manager and a general business manager or business analyst or IT manager), give them very little authority, and then put the job out to bid, select a few products and vendors, and go.

The project is understaffed, under budgeted, has no change management, and no involvement from any of the top leadership. The project fails and they wasted that budgeted 20%. They repeat this cycle a few more times, until they have spent 60% of what the project would realistically cost and still have no results. This is our audience for this book. Those leaders who have already burned 60%. Please keep reading, folks; you know who you are.

The top leadership of your organization needs to do the following:

- All the leaders must get behind the project passionately and enforce the change, making it clear to everyone that it is not optional.
- All the managers have to get tough with end-users who are dragging their feet or who have a wrong attitude or are engaging in bad behavior.
- All the leaders need to participate in change management activities, talking about the importance of the project often, emphasizing that it will succeed, that it is surely going to happen, and that it is a great endeavor which will ensure the future existence of the company.

- Bonuses and other incentives should be considered as a way to promote adoption of the new system by end-users.

To successfully usher in change, we need to prepare for change. That means communicating and championing the importance of the change, as well as reviewing and renewing your policies, business rules, workflows, and procedures, and cleaning up your master data before you even begin any IT project planning. The first Core Concept, **Embrace Change**, is all about making certain that you are properly prepared before you embark upon the details of planning the IT project itself.

The next Core Concept, **Seek Balance**, will ensure your project is properly planned by teaching you how to determine a realistic scope, phasing, and project management methodology.

Seek Balance

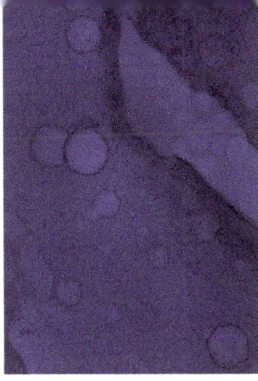

Introduction

In seeking balance, you must be humble enough to acknowledge that a new balance is needed; your current way of doing things is not working.

But what is balance? It's simply all parts of a larger whole functioning together and independently. In the case of an IT system upgrade, it's the right people and the right teams doing the right things at the right time. No outliers, no unnecessary resistance, no attempts for a quick fix, no sticking to the old ways because it's easy.

In Zen temples and centers, the master will occasionally disrupt the schedule and make new rules without any warning, so people don't become complacent. Such temporary imbalances help to keep things fresh and new. But it has a deeper purpose as well. In acclimating to periodic imbalances, one becomes able to find balance in the midst of imbalance.

When upgrading IT, of course, it's not merely about avoiding complacency. That could be accomplished by re-arranging meeting times and office spaces every now and then. An IT upgrade, on the other hand, is critical for productivity, efficiency, and perhaps even crucial for the survival of the organization.

Like monks and nuns in a monastery, corporate employees can become accustomed to doing things one way. Even if modes of work and processes are outdated and inefficient, there is a balance there that people might find

comforting. The workflow is predictable. There are no surprises and nothing to learn. But it's not a healthy balance. It's the balance of a stagnant pond. It's not the balanced flow of a vibrant river, one that fosters new life and movement and possibility.

If done properly, seeking balance can be liberating. Moreover, it is a process that includes jettisoning everything that is no longer necessary. And that can be liberating and exhilarating.

Layman Pang, a revered lay Zen practitioner in 8th century China, said famously: "How wondrous: my supernatural powers are chopping firewood and carrying water." Yes, if we can simply give ourselves to the task at hand, we find that there is no problem. It's only when we think we should be doing something else that problems arise. As Shakespeare's Hamlet famously put it, "I could be bounded in a nutshell, and count myself a king of infinite space—were it not that I have bad dreams."

This is the balance of mindfulness. In deep mindfulness, there is alignment of body, mind, action, and breath. There is a sense that it's all here. There's nothing missing and no need to compare or judge. There is no need to cling to things just because they're comfortable. There is no problem with temporary imbalances because it leads to a deeper and more enduring and resilient balance. Seeking balance does not feel extra; it's simply the natural impulse of an organization or team that recognizes the value in being nimble, responsive, and proactive.

There is a concept in Japanese culture called ichi-go ichi-e which means for this time only, and it's central in Zen practice. What needs to be done, the next step, is always right in front of us. It's just this moment. Just this breath. Just this step. Just this phase of the upgrade. And now just this phase.

As you'll see in the following section, the process and discipline of seeking balance can, and must, be gradual. It must be step-by-step, deliberate, and thoroughly thought through. Like koans, these and other concerns need to be considered carefully and deliberately:

- What's a realistic plan?
- Can all aspects of the scope of work be articulated?
- What's the minimal functionality needed?
- How clearly understood is the complexity of the current IT system?
- What would incremental progress look like?
- How will the process be managed? Who will need to do what?
- Do we have a good balance of IT professionals and management?

There is much talk about "the path" in Zen. One of the unique things about Zen is that the path ahead is clearly marked. The next step is always clear. In seeking balance with IT system upgrades, the path ahead must be fully planned out and understood by all. It is truly a "one step at a time" endeavor. The clearer the path, the easier it is to know when you're off-path and the easier it is to get back on track.

If you stick to what needs to be done next, there's no problem. It's when you get bogged down in abstractions, fear, and resistance—when your cup is overflowing with tea—that you get discouraged or despairing or think that you have all the answers.

At such a time, there's no room to learn or grow or evolve.

Seeking balance is finding that perfect middle ground, that ideal sweet spot between your most overly ambitious pie in the sky fantasy and your most cowardly minimal incremental tweak. If you earnestly take to heart and faithfully follow the first Core Concept, Embrace Change, you will be well prepared to take full advantage of this next Core Concept, Seek Balance. But even if you do a less than perfect job on change management, policy review, data cleansing, and other elements of Embrace Change, you can still have a fairly successful project just so long as you take this Core Concept, Seek Balance, very seriously.

The most important part of planning your IT project is coming up with a realistic, reasonable, practical, and feasible scope. Next you need to intelligently phase that scope in. Lastly, you need to manage all the many moving parts of the implementation.

This sounds really obvious.

1. Scope it. **Prune Our Garden**
2. Phase it. **Expand Our Territory**
3. Manage it. **Manage Our Miracle**

One would think that this is so obvious that it is not worth mentioning at all. Obviously, you need a realistic scope, a plan to phase the changes in over time, and a sensible project management methodology (which of course, these days means Lean and Agile). Why even talk about this? What's the big deal? Of course, this is so obvious, everybody has this covered. Surely, they must.

You would think…

You would be wrong, however.

This is the second quicksand death trap.

The first quicksand death trap is the complete lack of preparation we find when the first Core Concept, **Embrace Change**, is not understood and acted upon. We hope we have cured you of that blindness. You now know you should prepare for the planning; there is a pre-planning prerequisite which sets the stage for making the detailed plans. **Embrace Change** may be the most overlooked Core Concept of the Zen of IT. However, the heart of the Zen of IT is this second Core Concept, **Seek Balance**, where we teach you how to devise an intelligent and REALISTIC plan.

This second quicksand death trap appears when intelligent and experienced professionals (who should know better) behave like childish fools and underestimate the difficulty level of the terrain they are setting out to traverse. The root of the problem is always the same, underestimating the complexity of the existing IT system, and IT systems in general.

One reason for the lack of understanding of the complexity of the legacy system is that it is rarely documented. How can you understand the vast extent of all that your IT system entails when there is no write-up of it to speak of, not even a high-level overview? The system works (sort of) because each cog in each cubicle knows his or her own little bit of the dysfunctional dance of data in that silo, but there is nobody who understands how the whole thing works, and no way to learn it, fathom it, or wrap your mind around it, because there is nothing one can read that is comprehensive, intelligible, succinct, and up to date. There may be a few out-of-date swim lane diagrams that describe one tiny obscure process that is no longer relevant languishing in a dusty old SharePoint folder that nobody has visited in many years, but nowhere is there a comprehensive documentation of the legacy system which exposes all its terrible tentacles which reach out into the sordid sprawl of related applications, web portals, integration middleware staging areas, and finally dump their waste products into the dreaded dizzying array of disconnected, loose, and randomly named Excel files.

Your IT system is much more complex than you can ever imagine. Programmers understand this. Let me ask you this: when was the last time that a programmer planned an IT project? Never. IT projects are planned by managers, not coders. As one moves up the ranks to higher levels of IT management, one stops coding. One may lose sight of what it takes to make computers talk to each other. Other planners of IT projects include operational managers, software salespersons, consulting firm salespersons, partners or directors at CPA or IT consulting firms (whose primary role is sales), project managers, business executives, and sometimes an IT solution architect may have a small voice, which is sadly ignored. All of these folks in all of these roles tend to underestimate the difficulty of putting in a new system and they are in many instances guilty of hubris. If you remember only one thing from this entire book it should be this: get humble, bite off what you can chew, and chew it slowly, thoughtfully, and thoroughly before swallowing.

You must continue to operate the business during the implementation of the new system. It is like the concept of biological evolution. Life does not stop for even one second. You cannot freeze life for a dozen generations while you design a new organism from scratch and then release it into the world. The existing organism needs to evolve in slow stages in each generation while at the same time continuing to fight for survival in a hostile and competitive jungle full of predators and parasites. Likewise, your legacy IT system must evolve, surviving in an ultra-competitive marketplace, while you humbly and gently guide that evolution with intelligent, wise, and forward-thinking IT systems project planning.

You cannot simply replace the old system with a new system. I will say that again:

YOU CANNOT SIMPLY REPLACE THE OLD SYSTEM WITH A NEW SYSTEM.

(Or, worse yet, hire some consulting firm to do it for you and just leave it up to them.)

You are not changing the light bulb. You are not swapping out the hot water heater in your basement. You are not getting a new app where before you had none and just did it manually or in your head. You are overseeing the evolution of a complex silicon-based life form competing for survival in a hostile unpredictable and ever-changing business and governmental ecosystem. You are driving the bus in the movie Speed; if you stop the bus, it blows up and everybody dies. This is especially true if the IT system being replaced is the ERP system or impacts the ERP system in a major way, as in affecting super important things such as billing your customers, paying your vendors, shipping your products, paying your employees, or filing your tax returns.

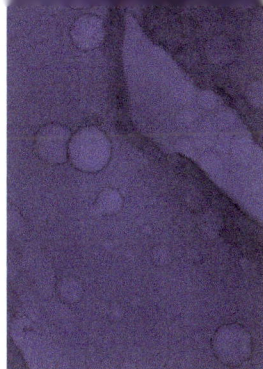

CHAPTER 4

Prune Our Garden

Master Nan-in served tea to a visiting scholar
who came to talk about Zen.

He poured his visitor's cup full, and then kept pouring.

The scholar yelled out, "It's full, stop!"

"Like this cup," said Nan-in,
"you are full of your own opinions and speculations.
How can I show you Zen unless you first empty your cup?"

Prune Our Garden

Putting in a new IT system is seen as an opportunity to greatly increase functionality and efficiency as well as to usher in a new world of automation that will reduce costs by reducing the number of administrative employees required to maintain the system. The thought is that the expensive shiny new system is going to be so much better than the dusty old system that as soon as it goes live it will start saving the organization tons of money, pay for itself within a year, and make everyone's job so much easier. After all, the software is very expensive, and the consulting fees to implement it are even more expensive. You reason that if I've spent all this money, I must be getting all this good stuff. If I am willing to spend a fortune to buy a Rolls Royce, I get a very well-made car that is immediately comfortable, fast, safe, and impressive. As soon as I drive it off the lot, it's great. Many people believe the same should follow for "buying" a new IT system.

However, as should now be clear from absorbing our first Core Concept, you cannot "buy" a new IT system, any more than you can purchase a new body. You might be able to get a heart, or a liver transplanted into your aging troublesome body, but you cannot get a full replacement for your entire physical organism. A business software application is a major organ in the organism of your overall IT system. You can't buy a new IT system for any amount of money. You can only repair the existing one. Your IT system is more than any one or two or three applications, no matter how monolithic they might seem. Your IT system is the business policies, the business rules, the business process workflows, the data integration programs, the internal and external application interfaces, the external reporting to shareholders and banks, the audited financial statements, the business intelligence managerial reporting, the operational reporting routines, the tax filings, the ad-hoc query capabilities, and so much more.

Replacing one or more applications is a way of repairing the existing living, breathing entangled system. Think of it as a heart transplant for an old man. Don't think of it as the birth of a new healthy baby. Unless you are implementing an IT system at a small start-up company, the biggest challenge of your business application implementation is fitting the new application into the existing morass of inter-related workstreams which have evolved into a complicated dystopian monster during decades of entrenched use, failed projects, and outright neglect. Over the years, your legacy system has grown long tentacles comprised of multiple applications, multiple departments, outside parties such as suppliers, customers, and governmental authorities, and is comprised not only of business software applications but also an avalanche of Outlook emails and Excel spreadsheets which exist as disconnected yet integral and critical steps in almost all of your business process workflows.

When your old ERP, CRM, industry-specific operational/billing system, or HR system was first introduced decades ago, the world was a different place. There were less integrations between applications and the internet was less ubiquitous. Nowadays systems are more entangled than ever before. Twenty or thirty years ago, it may have been somewhat feasible to replace an old ERP system with a new ERP system, for example. Today you cannot simply replace one system with another, you must also replace all the hooks it has into everything else. This is daunting, to say the least.

Please take this sage advice to heart: Lower your expectations. You have neglected your legacy IT system for decades. Now, your first step should be humble. As in, we are going to put in a modern cloud application which will have LESS functionality, LESS features, LESS bells and whistles, and be just barely enough to allow us to operate but will give us a solid platform on which to add functionality and efficiency over the ensuing years to eventually get us back to the level of functionality we enjoy today, and then ultimately surpass what we have now, because we will have the use of modern programming languages, expanded interface options, and increased scalability and performance, along with technical support from the software developer on a fully supported platform. We must ditch the old green screen application because it is not something viable to build a future upon. Sadly, we must lose the functionality of the forty-year-old green screen application as we usher in its weak new bare-bones replacement; nonetheless, this simply must be done to pave a way forward for our organization.

Rarely do business planners think in this humble manner. They are bold in their claims and loud in their insistence on how much better the new system will be and must be. If your existing IT system is an ancient relic from a bygone era, then realize that you have many years ahead of you of humble step-by-step improvements which will take a great deal of work, many years, and be very expensive. Do not believe that you can go shopping for a new app, then hire an authorized partner to implement it, then enjoy a beautiful new world of stunning efficiency in six months-time (or even 18 months). Just as a morbidly obese chain-smoker who spent decades as a heroin addict cannot suddenly join a really expensive fancy fitness club that has all the latest weight machines and swimming pools and enjoy great health day in 90 days, your entrenched outdated IT system cannot be rehabilitated in nine months.

The barest of minimal required functionality to run the business should be your only true requirements. Get out a machete and cut scope. Slash that scope out of the project ruthlessly and relentlessly. Strip that scope down to a naked little embryo. If you don't absolutely, positively, and completely need that feature or module to keep the lights on, get the orders out, and keep the doors open, then YOU DON'T REALLY NEED IT! Do you? Think of almost everything as phase two, phase three, phase four, or a future phase as yet to be determined. It's more than enough of an ambition to get rid of your horrible, outdated existing application.

Why do you think you are still running character-based applications on AS/400 or DOS applications or client/server applications that require Citrix or remote desktop connections or overly customized old versions of a major

ERP application which has become impossible to upgrade and is no longer supported? Why do you think you are in this unfortunate situation? Because in the past, every time you endeavored to swap out your old system, you were overly optimistic about scope, and the projects failed; hence, the system became more and more outdated as nothing got replaced over the years. Cutting scope to the barest of essentials is the secret sauce. Cut scope. Cut scope. Cut scope. And please, cut scope. Thank you.

Think of everything that is not truly essential to keep the business operating to a point where you can stay in business as a weed to be pruned out of your garden so that your tiny stub of a flowerless rose bush can establish itself and eventually bloom into its full potential as a strong plant with sharp thorns to protect itself and many sweet-smelling colorful flowers to attract busy bees. Think of the new application you are implementing as a sturdy little green stump with no flowers; the flowers (i.e., features) will grow later, during the continuous process improvement phase AFTER go-live.

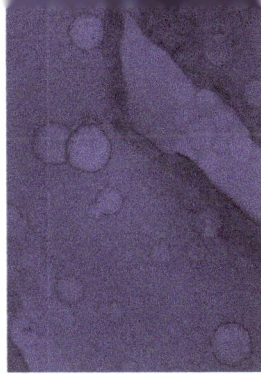

CHAPTER 5

Phase Our Journey

One day a monk declared that he wished to transcribe
the entire *Tripitaka* as his main work practice.

The head monk scoffed:
"How will you do that—it's thousands of pages long?"

"Easy," the monk said. "One page a day."

Phase Our Journey

We just talked about the paramount importance of cutting scope in the Core Concept Component, **Prune Our Garden**. Stripping requirements down to the barest of minimum required functionality is essential; however, even those Draconian measures are not enough. We need to go further. We need to delve into the deepest darkest center of the IT black hole and transcend the singularity. We need to talk about the big bang itself.

There are two approaches to IT system implementations: phased approach and big bang approach. The phased approach calls for gradual adoption whereas the big bang approach is a total replacement which occurs on go-live day. Why would anyone choose a big bang approach when obviously it would be much less risky and less disruptive to day-to-day operations to gradually adopt a new IT system, rather than for every process and everyone's job to change all at once, on one magic day? Why do they keep doing it? Why do C-level business executives, consulting firm partners, senior level IT solution architects, operations managers, and other otherwise intelligent people make the same stupid dreadful disastrous costly mistake over and over again of planning on an overly ambitious big bang go live?

The big bang approach is very seductive. Think of the big bang approach as a sultry temptress or a fast-talking used (I mean preowned) car salesman. The big bang approach is extremely tempting because it eliminates the very big, very real, gargantuan central problem of replacing your IT system. The reason that it is difficult to replace your IT system is because it is hooked into all your other IT systems and is an integral part of most of your operational workflows and reporting. With a big bang, everything changes all at once including all the sub-systems, subsidiary modules, related applications, custom reporting, and data integrations. Furthermore, if everything is being done all at the same time, we will only need to go through the implementation

methodology steps (discovery, analysis, detailed design, build, training, testing, etc.) just one time, not over and over again for each go-live phase.

The faulty seductive reasoning goes something like this: if I change everything simultaneously, then I won't have to create data integrations between the old as yet replaced pieces and the new pieces I am putting in; if
everything changes all at once, then the project will get done sooner and
we'll look like rockstars; if we just bite the bullet now, and do everything all
at once, then we will start getting the benefits of the new system years ahead
of time; if we go live with everything on the same day, then we won't have to
rack our brains to come up with a clever strategy as to how to phase it in; hey,
let's just swap in the entire new system now and get it over with, the sooner
the better.

When you phase in functionality, instead of adopting a big bang strategy, much of the old system remains in production during the initial phases,
and therefore, you have to build temporary data integrations which become
"throw away" code. Furthermore, with a phased approach, you have to be
very artful, clever, and creative, in thinking through how you are going to
phase in a piece of the system and work it into the existing morass of inefficient workflows which are the source of the pain points you have today.
The desire to bulldoze the entire legacy system and replace it all at once with
a fully integrated, modern system that is completely clean and clear of the
existing problematic jumbled manual workflows is very strong.

Now add to that the fact that the people selling you the software licenses
say it can be done, and claim that they do it all the time, and they don't bat
an eyelash, when you say you want to stand up their entire system on one
magical day which will occur in less than a year (despite the fact that it will
impact dozens, hundreds, or even thousands of people, who will all have start
using a brand new system all at the same moment on that one magical day).
Of course, they may not really believe that, at least not fully. They are just
telling you what you want to hear to get you hooked to an expensive annual

service contract that will become entrenched for decades to come. But don't blame them. They are just doing their jobs. You are to blame for backing the salespeople into a corner where they know full well that they stand no chance of getting your business unless they claim the big bang approach will work.

As unrealistic as a big bang may appear to even an overly optimistic fool, the phased approach appears worse. A phased approach is a hideous headache of tedious tiny steps, throw away code, and mind-melting conundrums of how to wedge the new pieces into the legacy mess, all needing to be borne with the patience of a saint. The big bang approach is glamorous, brave, glorious, gleaming, and wholly transcendent. The big bang approach is Shangri-La, El Dorado, and the Emerald City of Oz all rolled into one. The big bang is sexy and that is why people choose it over and over again (much to their peril). This is precisely the same reason why people fall for con artists and give away their life savings, because the offer is tempting and seductive; fools rush in where angels fear to tread.

The big bang approach is the better approach, but only if it would actually work, but the problem is that it rarely works. The big bang approach can work, but typically only if you have an immense budget and absolutely every aspect of your project is executed at optimal levels (which is almost never the case). It is not that the big bang approach always fails. There are cases where it succeeds, but in those cases, you are dealing with a tiny organization or a start-up company, or else you must be able to throw a tremendous number of resources at the project and orchestrate the change management perfectly.

Rarely works is not acceptable. These IT projects cost too much money, take too much time, and are a great risk as far as disrupting day-to-day operations, lowering morale, and possibly putting your company out of business. We should not roll the dice and hope that we are among the exceptions rather than the rule. The decision to take a big bang approach is THE MAIN RISK of failure for a large-scale IT project. Nonetheless, most large-scale IT implementations do take the big bang approach, and this is precisely why many of these projects fail, or at very least, fall far behind schedule. We have seen it over, and over, and over again.

We have also seen the big bang approach disguised as a phased approach. A true phased approach is phased by division, business unit, department, functional area, or software module. Phasing by location or worksite is not true phasing. Phasing by limiting the number of transactions such as including only the new transactions (new orders only) is not true phasing. Phasing by including only certain work locations or only new orders is just creating mini big bangs. You still need to create the entire new system in all its functional areas and then apply that only to a few locations or a few new orders. There is no complexity cut out and no time saved. There is less volume of transactions, true, and that may be helpful, but those transactions still need to flow through all the brand-new data pathways in every module and every department. Functionality is not truly phased, using that kind of strategy.

A true phased approach is the great approach, because each tiny phase is a humble little manageable step. It allows you to show steady progress. It is in line with Lean/Agile philosophy of breaking work into smaller chunks. Waterfall project management is considered dead and buried. Now please, let us all attend the funeral of the big bang approach.

For ERP implementations, for example, the order of phases could be as follows:

1. General Ledger
2. Financial Statements
3. Budgeting
4. Bank and Cash Management
5. Fixed Assets
6. Accounts Payable (Non-Trade Only)
7. Accounts Receivable (Invoice Header Only)

Those seven phases can happen without disrupting the overall operational system, such as a billing, inventory control, procurement, manufacturing, project accounting, timesheet capture, shop floor, warehouse management, field services, and time and billing. Once you get into the heart of the operational system, it becomes much harder to phase in pieces because those pieces are so tightly woven together. For example, inventory and procurement are very hard to tease apart; inventory items are listed on a purchase order. Nonetheless, by using integration programming you can even phase in among the tightly woven functional areas. For example, you could swap out a timesheet capture software first, then later have that same new timesheet capture system (workforce management system) point to a new billing system, but initially have it point to the old billing system. There are far too many possible options to discuss at length here, and the best course of action depends on myriad variables that are unique to each organization.

Even if you end up taking a big bang approach with the operational systems such as timesheets, inventory, purchasing, light manufacturing, shop floor or things of that nature, you could, nonetheless, start with a phased approach by slowly establishing a financial system beachhead. You can start by getting your accounting department acquainted with the new system through implementing the seven aforementioned purely financial modules first. Obviously, doing so will require throw away integrations as you will have to feed journal entries from the legacy subsidiary modules into the new General Ledger or feed accounts receivable transactions from the legacy billing system to apply cash to them, etc.

Standing up a new modern cloud-based general ledger as the official set of books for your organization and possibly redesigning your chart of accounts and financial statements would be a major accomplishment as a true phase one. You can demonstrate clear progress. Automating your non-trade Accounts Payable possibly using document imaging, artificial intelligence and workflow approval could be a huge early win. In this way, you can achieve early efficiency gains.

Having smaller scale successful go-lives along the way boosts confidence and lifts morale. The idea is to get your finance and accounting department on the new system first, including possibly the accounts payable and accounts receivable departments. Think of what it would mean to your likelihood of long-term success if cash management, financial statement preparation, non-trade (non-supplier) accounts payable and accounts receivable (cash receipts/ application) is well adopted and stabilized on new modern cloud-based services providing a stable base on which to expand your territory BEFORE you begin to tackle all the other more complex and densely intertwined functional areas such as purchasing, inventory, project accounting, manufacturing, and your operational systems along with the customer billing component. The accountants will already be up and running on the new system prior to all that more complex stuff having to be implemented.

Don't you see how daunting it is for EVERYTHING to change all at the same exact moment on one magical day?

Capture some tiny outpost of territory in the new cloud-based world. Conquer it. Stabilize it. Adopt it. Get your accountants or perhaps your HR department or perhaps your sales department on a new cloud-based IT system first. You can start with using CRM tools such as Salesforce, Microsoft Dynamics Customer Engagement, or some similar application, as a workflow tool to build end-to-end workstreams which cross functional and departmental areas. At first, those CRM workflows will have to tie-into the legacy ERP software, or legacy payroll system (if you haven't outsourced payroll yet), or legacy operational billing systems, or legacy field services or something else. However, once those new workstreams are in place, then later when the newer systems get implemented, you can re-point your CRM workflows to those newer systems without completely replacing them (although they will require extensive rework, of course).

This CRM example is one of many strategies for taking a phased approach. The options are limitless, but they all require ingenuity, creativity, vision, and lots of rework. The throw away code and rework turns many people off to adopting a phased approach. Do not be dissuaded by the inevitable rework inherent in taking a phased approach. The big bang approach is most often a complete disaster which requires the entire project to be scrapped, thereby losing several months or years and many thousands if not millions of dollars; sometimes people get fired or are forced to resign. So, ask yourself this: which is worse, throw away code, or a throw away career?

A prerequisite may be establishing a robust and powerful data integration middleware platform and/or business intelligence staging platform. Having powerful integration tools and a well-organized environment and tactical team that can create data integrations and perform data conversions, migrations, and ad-hoc reporting on your data is essential. You must have the ability to make the legacy system talk to the new pieces that you are adding. If at the outset of your major IT overhaul, you take the time and invest the money to build a well-oiled machine that can make applications talk to one another and to pull data out of an old system and transform it for the new system, then you will be much better prepared for the challenges that lay ahead when finally swapping out the legacy system in its entirety.

Asking the users to massage the data in Excel worksheets and labelling that a "data conversion" or a "data migration" is rarely sufficient and is an approach that should be taken only with very small and simple projects. It is truly amazing and very disheartening to witness how many IT project planners don't take data migration seriously and who believe that clerical users armed with Excel worksheets are the answer for uploading data into your new IT system; clerical users have neither the time nor the IT skills to properly de-duplicate, transform, and arrange data for loading new data and then keeping it in sync with multiple applications. A professional database programmer and data migration specialist is needed.

Phase Confusion

The word "phase" is used all the time when planning IT projects. However, this is a case where we need more words than just one. As the Inuit people have many words for the word snow, we need at least three words for the word phase. Features can be postponed to a later phase. Implementation methodologies call for implementation phases such as discovery, analysis, design, build, data migration, deploy, train, test, and post go-live support. Project plans are organized into project phases which are often lists of things such as lists of subsidiaries, locations, business units, divisions, applications, or software modules.

Features are not true phases, rather they should be thought of as continuous process improvement. If you say, "let's put those extra features in during a later phase" what you should be saying is "let's add that feature after go-live as part of our continuous process improvement planning." This is a crucial distinction. If you think that adding bells and whistles, nice-to-haves, and advanced features is a project phase or an implementation phase, then you don't understand phasing at all.

For every project phase, you need to complete all the implementation phases; this is a main confusion of IT systems implementation. To do this right, you must first separate the project into distinct project phases (as discussed earlier in this chapter). These are project phases and each of these is a "go-live". Each one of the individual project phases must go through the entire implementation phase lifecycle. Most people cannot handle that amount of planning and they don't have the patience to do it properly. The mistake that is often made (due to laziness, underestimating complexity, sheer ignorance, and being seduced by the big-bang fallacy) is that the "phases" of the project, mapped out in the project plan, are implementation methodology phases, and there are no distinct project go-live phases. If the project phases and the implementation phases are the same thing, with the same timeline, then obviously, what you are planning is a big bang in which all the functional areas and modules need to all go live miraculously on that one big magical day. Don't make this mistake. Instead have project go-live phases and for each project go-live phase break it out into each and every one of the implementation methodology phases.

Implementation methodology phases are usually not the problem with failed IT systems implementations. The implementation phases are very sequential, chronological, and unavoidable. You need a discovery phase which is high-level analysis and high-level scoping should follow next. Then you get into detailed design which should involve Agile iterative prototyping. Then you need to think about data conversion (also referred to as data migration), on-going integrations and interfaces, custom reporting, dashboards, third-party add-on products, train the trainer, user training, IT testing, user acceptance testing, cut-over planning, go/no go decision, go-live, and post go-live support. This book is not about implementation methodologies. Implementation methodology is rarely the problem, and many good books have been written on that subject.

This book is all about explaining why IT projects fail and saving you from that fate.

Hire IT system implementers with a proven track record; they will know the order of the implementation steps. They will have a rock-solid implementation methodology consisting of implementation phases. Make sure they have a proven track record with organizations in your size range. If you are their first big customer, run in the other direction. If you are self-implementing with your internal IT team, make sure that your internal IT team consists of experienced former consultants that know how to stand up new systems.

This book will teach you how to phase in the sense of the timing and scope of go-lives, because knowing how to do this (and knowing what not to do with regard to this) is the central wisdom of this book. This wisdom concerns what you are going to ask or demand that the implementers do (whether the implementers are internal or external or a combination of both). Most failures occur when top management requests and/or blesses a plan that is a "mission impossible". In these cases, although competent resources have been assigned to the project, because the project is simply not feasible to complete on its face value, it will be impossible for these resources to succeed, despite the fact that they are competent and hardworking individuals.

As IT consultants we have suffered under these mission impossible scopes too many times to recount. The scope is set by business owners, middle managers, executives, salespeople, CPA firm partners, consulting firm directors who arose from the sales ranks, and clerical users who have risen over the years to a level of top management. In other words, the scope is set by everybody other than people who have actually performed this kind of work before. Then later, after this impossible scope has been set in stone, the people who are actually going to perform the work step in. These folks are on a salary, and they have children to feed. They show up to work and they are afraid of losing their job. The impossible, illogical, and unrealistic plan is presented to them as a finalized signed sealed and delivered iron clad business contract already signed off by the C-Levels and legal departments of both firms. Now the IT consultants go into farce-mode and pretend that everything is okay when they know damn well the entire project is doomed from the start. They cannot speak up and ask that the entire scope be reworked, and that the fatally flawed strategy be turned on its head. It's too late. Speaking up will mean termination or becoming ostracized by being labelled as "unprofessional" or "not a team player".

This is the heart of this book. Getting that scope correct before the doers come into the picture and giving them something that they can actually do within the time allotted, budget provided, and the resources available.

If your organization is a conglomerate that is acquiring companies and stitching them together, then what a phased approach might seem to be to you is phasing in by acquired company. When formulating your plan, you must not lose sight that each company (or perhaps division or business unit) requires its own separate phased approach. Don't be fooled by the big bang approach disguised as a phased approach. Simply, calling each separate division or company a phase is not really using a phased approach. It may make more sense to run all or more than one of the implementations in tandem, but with each of them being phased within itself, rather than trying to pull off a sequential stream of big bangs. Then within each phase within each subsidiary are the implementation phases. It is phases within phases. Each go-live phase (i.e., project phase) has its own sequence of implementation phases.

Another way that the big bang approach masquerades as a phased approach is in feature reduction. As stated in the previous chapter, **Prune Our Garden**, it is essential to limit project scope to the bare bones minimal required features, and consider bells and whistles and nice-to-haves as later "phases". That being said, don't get confused here. People talk of feature "phases" which to be more precise should be labelled as really nothing more than continuous process improvement which occurs after a successful go-live project phase. Those aren't true project phases. By project phases we mean phasing in the go-lives, not phasing in additional features in the future pertaining to some piece which has already gone live. A project phase is a go live. A project phase is not merely an additional set of features added to an already live module. Each project phase must have all the individual implementation phases of discovery, analysis, design, etc.

It's relatively easy to phase in additional features. Where IT projects fail, get scrapped, and then require a very costly restart, is in cases where the new system never went live at all. The serious challenge is standing up a new application or module of an application in the real world without causing absolute mayhem within the organization. Continuous process improvement after go-live is how we eventually add in most of the time saving and money saving automation features.

First, we must reduce feature scope drastically to ensure that a new software module is actually able to go live and doing so provides a bare bones base to build on in the future. Secondly, we must reduce the number of software modules we intend to stand up on the same day by considering each module a project phase, because if we try to turn on all the modules at the same time, we are back to a big bang.

A module can also be thought of as a business functional area or even as a department; for example, a project phase could be the accounts payable (A/P) module or the A/P department or the A/P team because that project phase involves everything that needs to happen to get that group of folks to adopt the new system. In talking about reducing scope in the previous chapter we are talking about reducing features. Merely reducing features is not enough, we need to reduce departments, functional areas, and modules (all three of which can be roughly equated to the same thing).

A go-live does NOT have to be an entire application, and very often should not be. Applications have modules. Let's not confuse modules with features. Features are bells and whistles and nice-to-have features within a module. A module is a whole entire area of an application. For example, automatic application of cash receipts is a feature within the accounts receivable module of an ERP system. For example, guided data entry prompting is a feature inside of a CRM sales force automation module. For example, having fixed assets appear automatically (without double keying) in the fixed asset module based upon posting a receipt of goods transaction on a purchase order is a feature of the fixed assets module (that you can turn on or off depending on whether you are ready to enable it). Handheld barcode scanners is a feature inside a warehouse management system (WMS).

Workstream Extremes

In the IT world, there is a big push to stop talking and thinking in terms of departments and software modules. Speaking in terms of end-to-end workstreams, namely procure-to-pay (P2P), record-to-report (R2R), and quote-to-cash (Q2C) is in vogue. An end-to-end workstream is a business process that crosses departments, functional areas, business units, divisions, and even expands into affiliated companies and subsidiaries, vendors, customers, banks, and governmental agencies. To get everybody working together and on the same page, and functioning in the most efficient manner possible, we are told to design workstreams and think only in terms of the full end-to-end process when implementing software, writing up requirements documents, architecting new solutions, or advising clients. Management consultants who advise businesses and software companies that develop business software want to appear hip, up-to-date, and in-the-know, and they make a concerted effort these days to speak in terms of end-to-end workstreams and avoid using the old-fashioned terminology of "departments" and "modules".

All this emphasis on workstream vs. departments is valid in the sense that it is pointing out the need to tie together the processes that occur within a department with the parts of the process that occur outside that particular department. That being said, pretending that the lines between departments and modules don't exist or are an old-fashioned or passe way of organizing a business enterprise is counter-productive and frankly dangerous, because the fact remains that the most sensible way to phase in a project is to phase it in by department, meaning a functional area or a team or a software module.

Refusing to organize IT systems implementations by departments is foolhardy. Every sizable organization has an accounts payable department, an accounts receivable department, a controller in the accounting department, a sales department, a human resources department, a shipping area, a purchasing team, and so forth and so on. Organizations need to be ORGANIZED. Hence the term organization. Organizations are organized into departments (not workstreams). If they were organized into workstreams then every organization would have only three departments: procure-to-pay (P2P), record-to-report (R2R), and quote-to-cash (Q2C). Organizing your company into only three departments would be terribly inefficient because the three workstream departments would have too many people in them and would be unmanageable. We would be mixing apples and oranges as these different functional areas are each doing very different things. Furthermore, different types of personalities are needed in different types of departments; for example, people who are good at sales and marketing are probably best kept out of the accounting and payroll departments.

The way to resolve the stultifying problem of myopic siloed departmental fiefdoms is to build cross departmental end-to-end workstream-oriented workflows and intelligent and well-designed automated data integrations between departments and software application modules, not pretend that there are no separate departments and there are no separate software application modules.

There are departments and there are software modules, and guess what? They are not going away any time soon, and that's a good thing. Learn to phase in by department and module. This is the true phased approach. Do not phase by features. Do not phase by whole applications. Do not phase by whole subsidiaries. Do not phase by entire end-to-end workstreams involving dozens of departments. The module or functional area or department must go live first. Then as a continuous process improvement, you can add automation (if it does not already come as an out-of-the-box feature) that enhances or in some cases allows for the flow of shared information (without re-keying) between the modules and departments.

Embrace the idea of phasing by the go-live date of one or more software modules (which generally speaking, equates to a departmental functional area going live on the new IT system). This is the heart of the true phased approach, not to be confused with all of the false so-called phased approaches.

False So-Called Phased Approaches

- Phasing by Software Feature Set

- Phasing by Entire Application
- Phasing by Entire Business Entity
- Phasing by Limiting to Only New Transactions
- Phasing by Limiting to Only Certain Site Locations

What these false so-called phased approaches have in common is that they are big bang approaches in disguise. They call for turning on every single module across all departments all at the same time. Attempting to go live on every module and every department all at once is a very bad idea in most cases.

People choose these false phased approaches because it's very easy to make a list of features, a list of apps, a list of divisions, a list of site locations, and then call that your phases and slap on some go-live target dates pulled out of thin air. Done. You have finished your brilliant design. The only problem is that it won't work.

The true phased approach requires creativity and deep thought because you have to start thinking about the DETAILS of what you are actually dealing with, not just a simple laundry list. People can sometimes be too lazy to delve into the details, or they have the opposite problem in that they get lost in the weeds. To design an intelligent and effective phased approach, you need to plan at a high level, but not too high a level where you don't really understand what's involved. The level you need to think at is the module and departmental level. The application level is too high. The business entity level is too high. On the other hand, the feature level is too low. The site location level is often irrelevant if it involves also thinking only in terms of the entire application. A modular / business functional area phase in requires an understanding of how to assess, scope and design accurate and reliable data integration programs, most of which will be throw away code. Because few know how to design or program good integration programs, most people don't want to phase by module. They end up going with the big bang.

What happens to many big bangs?

Many big bang projects drag on, and on and on and on... Here is how it goes. They set a ludicrously early go-live date; even the person setting it knows it's not reality. Three months prior to that, they ask for another month, then another month, then one more month. Then there is a "come to Jesus" meeting to explain the extenuating circumstances and they ask for another nine months. Now the planners actually believe they can do it. After all, they have a whole giant swath of nine fresh months.

But what they don't realize is that they could be granted another nine years, and it wouldn't matter one tiny bit. Their big bang approach cannot work no matter how long they have, because the business is changing and evolving during these long expanses of time and hence the requirements are always a moving target.

Because they did not limit the chunks of work to small pieces that they could go live with predictably and within a matter of a few months, nothing has gone live nor will anything ever go live; therefore, they have nothing to show, and will never have anything to show for all their work and money wasted. Because nothing ever goes live, they never provide anything stable to build upon. They have failed to capture a beachhead and then expand their territory in increments. They fall into a cycle of asking for an extra month a few months before each missed big bang go-live date, which they do a few times, followed by yet another major project reorganization which comes with another big ask for a "final" stretch of several months.

When it finally becomes clear to the poor hapless souls who are paying for all this and getting nothing in return, the entire project is scrapped. The big bang ends up being nothing more than a big, long, slow bust. The clerks click away at their dumb terminals as their faces glow happily in the light of the green screen. They inch closer to retirement sure in the knowledge that these fools will never swap out their beloved legacy system which predates HAL from 2001 A Space Odyssey. They will retire to the noisy clicking and clacking of a dot-matrix printer which will be sweet music to their aged ears.

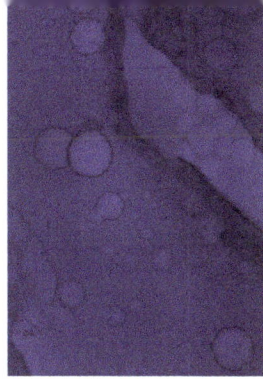

CHAPTER 6

Manage Our Miracle

A monk asked the Master:

"Why do some practitioners fail to make progress in their realization of the Way while others make it seem so easy?"

The Master said, "Like practitioners, there are four types of horses. The first type of horse never learns, even if whipped and goaded repeatedly. The second kind of horse only moves when it feels the pain of the whip. The third kind of horse runs at the lightest touch. The fourth type of horse moves at the mere shadow of the whip."

Manage Our Miracle

Project management is essential and Lean and Agile project management methodologies are far better than the traditional waterfall approach. Good project managers are rockstars. A good project manager is an artist, a scientist, and a sage. Make sure you have top-notch project managers and follow a Lean and/or Agile methodology. Please do this. However, do not think that the way to successfully implement a new IT system lies in project management alone. Project management is just one part of the story.

The big problem today is that IT systems pundits and business leaders alike are professing that Lean and Agile project management is the surefire and sole cure-all for failed IT systems implementations, but they are mistaken. The reasons why IT projects fail are the reasons given in this book. And those reasons are not limited to project management, and in fact, most of them don't involve project management. There is so much over emphasis on Lean and Agile these days that it has become akin to a cult-like obsession.

The faulty logic goes something like this: the IT project failed, it cost us millions of dollars, and we have nothing to show for it. What went wrong? What should we do? Answer. The project was mismanaged and therefore, obviously, the answer is better project management and more emphasis on project management.

No. No. Nooooooooooooooooooooooooooooooooo!!!

The answer is better MANAGEMENT, not better project management.

IT projects fail because of management failure or bad consulting advice, not project management failure. There is a difference. Management is more than just adopting and adhering to a Lean and/or Agile project management methodology. Management is high-level decision making, leadership by example, balancing day-to-day operations with IT systems implementations, high-level strategy regarding business policies and operational strategy, laying down the law with underperforming or ill-behaved employees, and knowing what is possible (by getting sound advice from vetted consultants) within the limits of budgetary and time constraints. Some of these management duties may be undertaken in the context of participating in a project or initiative which is undertaken using a Lean and/or Agile project management methodology, but much of it takes place outside of the project management realm.

Project management is managing projects and Agile project management is a project management methodology which arose out of software developers needing to better control the creation of software. For software developers, creating software is day-to-day operations, but for all other organizations there is a day-to-day operational reality that is more critical than as well as outside of IT. For software developers Agile project management methodology is the end-all and be-all because all they do is develop software; that is their core business. Not so for everybody else. Lean methodology was developed by the Toyota Motor Corporation as a way to improve a manufacturing assembly line. The odds are that your organization is neither a software developer nor an automobile manufacturer.

Most organizations suffering from wasteful IT spending, are wasting money on their attempt to adopt an already coded software application, not failing in their efforts to code commercial software or build cars on an assembly line. The audience for this book are managers (not necessarily project managers) that are struggling in their efforts to get their organization to adopt already finished and perfectly serviceable business software platforms and suffering setbacks because they don't understand the pitfalls of business software implementations that are explained here in this book.

These pitfalls are exposed and explained here without having to adhere to the cult-like buzzword-laden jargon of the Lean / Agile craze which has become its own cottage industry and is now seeking to expand itself to the point where it becomes management itself, not just project management. Lean / Agile will never succeed in consuming all of management because management is too huge a topic to be contained in any one methodology, no matter how popular, and especially because the Lean / Agile methodologies were devised by computer programmers or car manufacturers for very specific purposes, namely for developing computer programs or building cars, meaning these two incompatible methodologies do not apply to all initiatives, all day-to-day operations, all industries, all cultures, and absolutely everything your organization does and to the totality of everybody's job. Lean / Agile is a good methodology but should be applied judiciously and with reasonable expectations about what it can achieve.

IT systems implementations do not fail ONLY because of bad project management, and in fact, rarely do they fail due to poor project management; it is usually something else.

Here is a common scenario. The IT systems implementation failed. However, the project was run using an Agile methodology which was expertly executed. The Agile ceremonies all took place on schedule. The Agile artifacts were duly signed off on. The scrum master protected his team from the ruthless product owner making for a healthy equilibrium of checks and balances. The daily standups were well attended and very collaborative. The sprint retrospectives were enlightening and constructive. The project was managed perfectly and using all the latest Lean and Agile tools including a well-designed and expertly implemented Jira Software platform. However, the project failed miserably. How could this be?

The Agile methodology tells you how to break up the work into manageable chunks and collaborate successfully building positive feedback loops. However, at a very high level you can still fail miserably at basic common sense. As you read in the last chapter, **Phase Our Journey**, the big bang approach is a seductive trap that Agile will not save you from unless you become aware of it. The big bang trap is the main reason large-scale IT implementations fail, not faulty project management.

Furthermore, neither Lean nor Agile methodology specifically addresses the confusion between workstreams and departments and modules, nor does it distinguish between the different types of phasing. Lean and Agile does not directly address the problem of a big bang approach disguised as phased approach, although it could be argued that it does address all of the scoping problems in its underlying philosophy. However, this book highlights these pitfalls in a very direct manner, and that is precisely what is desperately needed in today's IT world.

As you read in the first chapter, change management is its own discipline which is distinct from project management, and neglecting change management is another major pitfall. This important consideration has nothing to do with project management per se. Change management is a completely separate yet very apropos topic.

The first Core Concept, **Embrace Change**, emphasizes the amount of pre-planning and preparedness required BEFORE planning should even commence for your IT projects, whereas Agile teams usually start work after many high-level bad decisions have already been made and after it's too late because the underlying policies and business rules of your organization have never been seriously questioned or examined, nor was there any effort to cleanse your data. Your users may have been granted too much say, too much veto power, and too much responsibility for data conversions, coding schemes, data cleansing, and system design in the IT systems implementation, and Agile will not only not address that error but may actually exacerbate it as Agile project managers seek to involve the users in their project methodology to keep them under the Agile umbrella. However, because these users are clerks using an off-the-shelf app, not programmers coding commercial software, the inclusion of them in the various Agile ceremonies may not bear much fruit.

The round peg / square hole shoehorning of Agile from software development to the completely different animal of getting clerical users to adopt a shrink-wrapped application has gone too far. Agile was designed for efficient collaboration between small groups of software developers who are creative mathematically oriented technical computer experts busily coding features into existing code bases and trying to meet their target code release dates; doing this comprises the entirety of their day-to-day responsibilities. What does that have to do with getting clerks to adopt a new order entry system or an accounts payable module while under immense pressure to keep up with day-to-day transactions and customer demands? To be honest, very little.

Picture this scenario. An order entry clerk in the midst of busy season and during an interruption of the supply chain struggles through the daily storm of their day-to-day operational responsibilities which is mainly comprised of urgent and critical ad-hoc tasks none of which are part of the new IT system implementation project. The clerk's activities include responding to emails or making phone calls or updating Excel spreadsheets which are not part of any software application legacy or new. As the clerk desperately struggles to keep up with the emails, phone calls, and spreadsheets, he or she is told to attend a scrum retrospective. Scrum is just some weird buzzword to them. It means absolutely nothing to them. To them it is a stupid management meeting which is a waste of their precious time, and indeed it often is. Top management can feel secure that they will not become outdated or put out to pasture because they are hip, with it, and cool as they are evangelizing the Agile doctrine within their organization. But meanwhile, the multi-million dollar IT system implementation is failing because it is a big bang in disguise which has absolutely zero chance of success.

Agile has not saved you and Agile will not save you in these kind of scenarios. IT systems implementations are still failing in droves. It is time to heed the simple no-nonsense wisdom contained in this book and stop over emphasizing project management as the silver bullet and panacea for everything that is wrong in the world.

If you want to win the World Cup, the World Series, the Superbowl or a gold medal at the Olympics, you must have a top coach, with a great strategy, and a competitive modern training methodology. But the coach does not win you the championship, the players do. The coach is part of the story. Lean and Agile project management is part of the equation, not the whole equation. If we keep adding project managers and place too much emphasis on project management that will hurt the project, not make it succeed. If we institute ceremonies and use fancy jargon and buzzwords in our business meetings that will not help us one tiny bit.

The advances in project management brought about by Lean and Agile methodologies are very helpful and should be adopted. And let's face it, nothing we write in this book is going to slow down that bandwagon. The odds are that your next IT project will be managed using a Lean and/or Agile methodology. That's all well and good. No problem there. But now let's move on to identifying the real reasons why large-scale IT implementations fail so that we can avoid making those mistakes.

We don't need more project management, rather we need management to hire more IT people. We need management to compel and encourage users to adopt the new system. We need management to stop getting seduced by the big bang fallacy. We need management to examine the polices and business rules of the business years before we even think about changing our IT systems. We need management to champion change, pay for change management consultants, take change management seriously, and to lead by example and get deeply involved in IT systems implementations, instead of hedging their bets by staying out of the fray and hiding behind layers of middle management scapegoats.

Mostly we need people who can do the actual IT work. Guess what? Those people are not project managers nor are they the end-users (often referred to as subject matter experts). IT systems are implemented by professional IT systems implementers. The more IT talent you bring to bear on a project, the more likely you are to be successful. Hire top-notch IT talent both internally and externally. Support them when they complain about end-users or middle managers who are hampering the project or trying to expand the scope by including every single nice-to-have. And please, don't burden them with an over emphasis on project management to the point where the project management methodology becomes an end unto itself.

Sometimes these IT projects morph into surreal nightmares in which one computer programmer is trapped in a small room with a half dozen project managers who are asking her why the tasks are not finished. The programmer asks to be let out of the room to get back to her desk to do the tasks, and this very reasonable and logical request is denied. The project management methodology requires that the meeting be held and take a certain amount of time and that these statuses get updated and status reports get distributed on time, even though the software will not. So much time is spent in serving the project management methodology that there is little to no time left to do the actual IT work and there are few people involved in the project who are skilled enough, technical enough and actually capable of doing good IT design work or successfully configuring or coding software applications. Mostly it's managers holding lengthy meetings with users and debating what features the software should include. These interminable meetings are conducted without a skilled IT person present to explain to both managers and end-users the unfeasible nature of their erroneous ideas.

Let's see just how much the Agile Manifesto does not apply to the adoption of new software platforms at an organization, adoptions which may involve an ERP, CRM, or ECM implementation which requires design work, application configurations, infrastructure changes, custom coding, selection of add-on modules, data cleansing, data migration, on-going data integrations, one-time data loads, and more. These are the typical IT projects that fail, resulting in lost time and money.

Agile Principle 1

Our highest priority is to satisfy the customer through early and continuous delivery of valuable software.

If you consider the "customer" to be the application end-users at your organization, then this principle is fine. Keep in mind that they use the word "customer" instead of "user" because these principles are geared toward a software developer's customers buying commercial software. They actually mean "buyers."

Agile Principle 2

Welcome changing requirements, even late in development. Agile processes harness change for the customer's competitive advantage.

Agreed. We should not freeze requirements long before the system is ready for deployment (like they used to do forty-years ago when designing monolithic COBOL-based mainframe applications).

Agile Principle 3

Deliver working software frequently, from a couple of weeks to a couple of months, with a preference to the shorter timescale.

This is false in many circumstances. You may be working in the analysis implementation phase and be conducting current state analysis of the legacy system. In that case your deliverable (i.e., evidence of progress) is an as-is study which is a Word or PDF document with swim-lane process flow diagrams, or information entered into some other application you are using to store the as-is study, such as DevOps or Jira Confluence. You will NOT be delivering any software, perhaps for six months. When you are writing software, then yes, it makes sense to deliver software. When you are implementing and adopting software, it often does not.

Agile Principle 4

Businesspeople and developers must work together daily throughout the project.
This is true in a software development company where you need to keep the developers in touch with the sales team to ensure they are making products that can be sold. This statement is false in the case of most software platform adoption and implementation projects. The business does not need to engage with IT every single day. You need to interview and observe users to see what they are actually doing in the trenches on a day-to-day basis and understand their pain-points and wish-lists, but then you go away and design a solution, meeting only to present a slide deck, a functional design document, screen mock-ups, and prototypes for the purpose of getting feedback. You should meet often and follow an iterative approach, but it is certainly not every day. Getting the businesspeople intimately involved in the actual detailed design work stalls the project and can easily derail it. Neither managers nor clerical end-users design IT systems for a living; therefore, they don't know how to do it.

Agile Principle 5

Build projects around motivated individuals. Give them the environment and support they need and trust them to get the job done.
Very true.

Agile Principle 6

The most efficient and effective method of conveying information to and within a development team is face-to-face conversation.
This is false. Unstructured conversations (whether in person or via video conference) are the main reason why IT systems design meetings are typically inefficient, bear little fruit, and lead to failed implementations. This topic

is discussed in detail in the Core Concept Component, Meet to Act. You need to convey useful information which is exactly what is needed to make progress. That information should be clear, ordered, and precise functional and technical specifications which are WRITTEN DOWN. The typical problem with IT systems implementation is that all the chatter that takes place verbally in so-called design meetings is not captured and is not acted on. Even if the video conference is recorded, the recording would still need to be paraphrased into some definitive next steps. Too much blabbering goes on in meetings with no concrete results. To give people a license to do more of it is not going to improve your results.

Notice that this principle says, "within a development team" not "within a project team". What this principle is really saying is that you should get your software coders (who are solitary anti-social computer nerds for the most part) out of the cubicles and away from the email chains and into a conference room to hash things out verbally, because these tech junkies are likely to over-use non-verbal communication.

Agile Principle 7

Working software is the primary measure of progress.

This is false when talking about implementation vs. development; otherwise, it certainly is true. When you are implementing and adopting one or more new software platforms at your organization as part of a digital transformation, the software already works as soon as you log into your cloud-based app. However, you don't know what switches in the setup that you should flip. It's a configuration issue. You don't know what kind of data feeds you need to put in place. You haven't designed your business process workflows to take advantage of the new features and capabilities already included and coded in the new apps. The primary measure of progress is NOT working software. The primary measure of progress is peer-reviewed non-boilerplate functional and technical design artifacts. These artifacts can be PowerPoint,

Visio, Excel, Word, PDF, or information in DevOps or other applications used to document your design. These artifacts don't need to be old-school rigid specification Word templates. That being said, the primary evidence of progress is good design artifacts. Without those artifacts you cannot build a decent prototype in the sandbox environment.

Agile Principle 8

Agile processes promote sustainable development. The sponsors, developers, and users should be able to maintain a constant pace indefinitely. The reason this principle was created is because software development was notoriously inefficient and developers would come up against do-or-die deadlines (usually having promised the venture capitalists the code would be ready by a certain fiscal quarter) and then everyone would have to go into round-the-clock crunch mode to get it done, as in cramming for final exams in college.

If you are working efficiently, you should not have to cram, then take long breaks of idleness, then cram again falling into a dysfunctional cycle of last-minute heroics.

Agile Principle 9

Continuous attention to technical excellence and good design enhances agility.
This is very generic and obvious. Pay attention to your technical and functional design. We agree.

Agile Principle 10

Simplicity—the art of maximizing the amount of work not done— is essential.
This is very true for IT systems implementations as well as software development. This is precisely the first Core Concept of The Zen of IT. This is our

Core Concept Component #1, **Simplify Our Lives**, but it is also at the heart of most of our other Core Concept Components as well.

Agile Principle 11

The best architectures, requirements, and designs emerge from self-organizing teams.

This is also true for IT systems implementations. The reason this is true is that different circumstances present varied mixes of human resource availability and IT system requirements. The makeup of teams will have to vary depending on what needs to get done, who is available, and what skillsets they bring to the table. For example, some people can do business analysis, functional design, and technical design, whereas others may be effective at only one of these roles. Some people are great coders but should not be put in front of the end-users or clients, because you'll have an awkward standstill. This is why the teams should be allowed to self-organize rather than starting with a rigid mindset of how many people should be on each team and exactly what their roles should be confined to.

Agile Principle 12

At regular intervals, the team reflects on how to become more effective, then tunes and adjusts its behavior accordingly.

In Agile, those regular intervals are typically set at every two weeks to be timed with the end of a two-week sprint. However, rarely do serious work issues and readjustment of roles and responsibilities need to be ironed out every two weeks. Hence, what happens is that an hour or two of everyone's life is wasted going through the ceremonial ritual of wracking your mind to come up with "what went right" and "what went wrong" in the last two weeks. Instead, what should happen is that if there are issues that one or more people have about how the team can be made to work more harmoniously or efficiently, then there should be a mechanism in place to voice those concerns. Another option is to space the "retrospective" ceremonies out to every quarter or maybe once a month (if that). This principle is a perfect example of how "Agile" can devolve into a bureaucratic, onerous, charade, where useless ceremonies are suffered through by people who have work to do and would rather just attend to their work.

The Four Agile Values

Individuals and interactions over processes and tools.
Agile methodology once adopted at your organization itself becomes a standard and formal "process" of how to work collaboratively. Let's listen to this value and take it to heart that adhering to the Agile "process" is not really all that important. What is more important is to value individual human beings and let them naturally interact. These human beings cannot be created with cookie cutters like gingerbread people and housed in pigeonholes. Vet first, and then hire top IT talent and let them do their thing. Demand evidence of their work along the way. Make sure that your IT system overhaul project plan is a phased approach with clear and concrete milestones. These rules of thumb are far more important than knowing that people have attended a recurring meeting no matter how fancy the label you've attached to that recurring (i.e., annoying, and often pointless) meeting.

Working software over comprehensive documentation.
Yes, obviously if the software doesn't work, you can't go live. Nonetheless, a major problem with IT transformation is that the legacy system isn't documented at all making the as-is study much more time-consuming and therefore expensive to conduct. Another problem that stems from lack of documentation is that the cost of maintaining the system increases due to the inefficiency of tech support having to reverse engineer the existing system almost every time something goes wrong, instead of quickly looking up how

the system is configured currently using up-to-date and fairly comprehensive documentation. Any breadcrumb trail at all will be a huge help to existing tech support staff as well as to consultants coming in to design a new system and first seeking to understand the current state of the legacy system. The LACK of documentation is a huge problem in most cases, rather than too much emphasis on documentation. Furthermore, the value itself says "over" and not "instead of". Too many people are using this "value" as an excuse to be sloppy, lazy, and disorganized in the sense of lacking sufficient IT systems documentation. As you will read in our last Core Concept Component, Write to Read, IT documentation artifacts are the primary measure of progress and absolutely fundamental to IT system design. In other words, the design document is the design (along with prototypes).

Customer collaboration over contract negotiation.
This value is about the sales cycle from the perspective of the seller. However, in most cases, your organization is the buyer. Again, this does not really apply to what you are likely to be doing regarding your IT systems overhaul.

Responding to change over following a plan.
The problem of project failure on large-scale IT systems digital transformation projects is not that we are rigidly and stubbornly sticking to a fixed plan. The problem is that our plan is seriously flawed and that we didn't do any pre-planning. The plan itself is bad because it's not a true phased approach that is reasonable, doable, and realistic given the budgetary and time constraints. THAT IS THE MAIN PROBLEM: UNREALISTIC PLANS! Again, this value won't help you with regard to implementing a new IT system at your organization. This value will help software developers get code out the door quicker, which is precisely why it was adopted as a value in the Agile software developer's manifesto.

Act as One

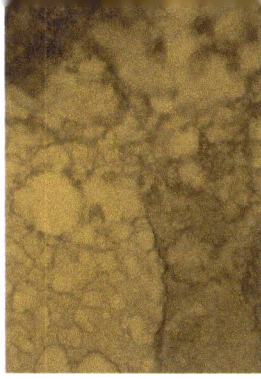

Introduction

As the Zen teacher Shunryu Suzuki famously said: "In the beginner's mind there are many possibilities, in the expert's mind there are few."

It's impossible to know all downstream implications of every phase in a major IT change. Communication is key. Open minds, deep listening, and good questions win the day by bringing and keeping people on the same page.

To act as one at the organizational level means everyone has something at stake. Everyone feels ownership and everyone has a voice. Everyone can contribute and everyone is encouraged to contribute. Upper-level management is involved and enthusiastic. This means, of course, that upper-level management must take responsibility for problems.

When leaders take responsibility for mistakes, delays, and misunderstanding, and then share or deflect success, four things tend to happen:

1. Leadership, and the process itself, earns trust.
2. Teams are strengthened.
3. Others are inspired to take responsibility.
4. Team culture becomes more cohesive when it's clear that it's OK (and sometimes necessary) to make mistakes.

There is a famous Zen story about the cook of a monastery who inadvertently cut off the head of a snake in the garden and cooked it in the otherwise vegetarian soup. When the master called the cook over during the meal and asked him about the head of the snake floating in his bowl, the cook immediately scooped out the head with his own spoon, and immediately ate it.

The cook not only takes full responsibility; he is decisive and efficient in his response. This is how meetings, and the entire phased upgrade should be run: with decisiveness, personal responsibility, and efficiency. **Ask yourself:**

- What's the agenda?
- Is there a snake head that I need to eat?
- What's the next step?
- What will it look like in three months if we're making progress? In six months?
- How can we demonstrate proof of progress?
- Do we have milestone deliverables clearly articulated and understood?
- Where's the documentation & who's responsible for managing it?
- Is there transparency; can anyone have access to the documentation?
- Is there regular and full reporting?

In their involvement, upper-level management must not hold themselves aloof; they must be willing to do whatever work is necessary, shoulder-to-shoulder with everyone else. In many Zen temples, the master is sometimes given the job of cleaning the toilets. But don't misunderstand it's not a teaching about staying humble. The import is much deeper. Work is work. Any judgments one has about a task are just that: judgments that we create. Fictions. In cleaning the toilets, the Zen master is also demonstrating another deep truth: we are one team here. There is no one fundamentally above or below anyone else.

Another tradition in Zen temples is samu: work as spiritual practice. This is a concept almost completely unknown and even totally rejected in the West with its obsession with work versus life balance. But in Zen, work, even something mundane like washing dishes, can be a powerful vehicle for letting go of ego (me, my, mine) and merging with something measureless. In washing dishes with no resistance, there is no problem. One might even find it miraculous: the dishes are washing the dishes. As taught at the Upaya Zen Center in New Mexico: "If we are cleaning up after dinner, that is the task at hand. When we indulge the various stray thoughts that come up, such as "I'm tired," or "Someone else should do this," we divide our effort and prevent unity."

Uniting a team with a single focus and purpose has benefits that go way beyond the quantifiable success of an IT upgrade. Teams and indeed, whole departments and companies, report a deepened and long-lasting sense of camaraderie, purpose, accomplishment, when there is a successful large-scale project completion.

If you follow all the principles explained in this book, your next major IT initiative will succeed. Even though IT systems are extremely complicated, and replacing one is akin to changing the tires on an eighteen-wheeler delivery truck as it continues to race down the highway already late to its next appointed destination, as long as you come up with a reasonable and feasible scope and hire enough qualified IT professionals to tackle those limited chunks of work and set realistic timeframes, then you will have no major problems. Your next IT system implementation will be a happy string of boring go-lives.

Let's get our bearings here. If we are following the principles of The Zen of IT, we have taken change management seriously and invested in it.

We have a change management strategy in place. Top management is unified in championing the IT systems digital transformation project. We have established a data lake or data warehouse and staging area in which we can programmatically manipulate large data sets. We are not using Excel spreadsheets as our primary means to conduct data migrations. We have established a data integration middleware platform so as to be able to build bi-directional bridges between the legacy live production system and slowly phased in functional areas and software modules. We have data migration and data integration experts (internal resources or external consultants) who can migrate data as one-time loads as well as design, program, test and monitor on-going feeds. We have cleansed our data to the best of our ability far in advance of making a detailed project plan. We have examined our organization's policies and business rules such as sales commission schemes, bonus calculations, customer discount and rebate schemes, number of separate business entities having separate sets of accounting books, fixed asset capitalization thresholds, and more, and done all of this far in advance of planning our digital transformation. We have had the courage, the will, and the authority to officially alter our organization's policies so as to drastically simplify our business rules wherever possible BEFORE embarking on our digital transformation. We are avoiding the trap of paying a fortune to try to create an unnecessarily complex IT system to meet so-called requirements which are really nothing more than a lack of examining and simplifying our policies. We have prepared ourselves to begin to plan our large-scale IT implementation project.

In planning the project, we have reduced the scope of features of each individual functional area down to the bare bones essential true requirements. We have adopted a true phased approach, not a big bang in disguise. We understand that a phase is a go-live, not additional features added to an already live system. We plan to slowly phase in by functional area or software module, despite the fact that such an approach calls for throw away integration coding and headache-inducing creative thinking. We understand that phasing by location or by only putting through new orders in the new system is a big bang in disguise because as long as the entire business process workstream traversing all the functional areas has to be stood up, we will need to design, configure, customize, test, and train on all those functional areas all on one day (which is the problem with the big bang approach), even if the only thing we plan to run through that workstream is one single solitary transaction.

We understand the benefits of Lean and Agile project management and have adopted it. We also understand that these project management methodologies, while certainly good for our projects, are not the end-all and be-all and the answer to all our woes. We know that calling a meeting a scrum instead of a meeting is just playing around with buzzwords. We must implement Lean and Agile where it makes sense to do so and truly use those methodologies, not just be up to our same old tricks, and using a different terminology in our Outlook meeting invite subject headers. We realize that project managers are super important, but that the actual hands-on work is done by functional application experts and technical IT resources such as software engineers, database programmers, and the like, and we cannot win the game without enough top IT talent brought to bear on the project.

IT projects fail because people fail to face reality. Suckers are stripped clean of their money by con artists because they fail to face reality. If the low-dollar investment was such a fantastic opportunity then the con artists hawking it would not be wasting their time struggling to sell it to you, they would simply invest in it themselves. Likewise with IT project planners, they need to face reality; they cannot pull off massive, big-bang projects with limited resources, insufficient budgets, and accelerated timeframes, no matter what project management methodology they employ.

In our second Core Concept, Seek Balance, we cleared up the confusion people have with project phases. Understanding how to specify what is truly an achievable chunk of work, how long it should take to get done, how many people are needed, and what skill sets they should have, is both an art and a science. You need to hire professional IT system architects who can put that kind of plan together for you. Too often the plan is devised by high-level managers who are not IT system designers. The IT system professionals are brought in too late in the process, handed a mission impossible assignment, granted very limited authority, and the entire project is doomed to failure from the start.

To make matters worse, many so-called IT system professionals are incompetent. They should know how to scope a project that is reasonable, feasible, logical, and doable, but they don't because they fall into the same traps that upper management does, such as the big-bang fallacy, failing to understand that they need to phase by functional area and software module, and underestimating the complexity of the legacy system, among other errors. Too many IT system "professionals" have been misleading clients for years, and getting away with it, because they can parrot all the right buzzwords and appear knowledgeable, but unfortunately are neither competent nor trustworthy. Don't be naive. Be wary. You have to find people who are known quantities with proven track records through word of mouth. Don't be blinded by the buzzwords, nor by the credentials, nor by software certifications of people you just recently met and don't really know. Vet everyone.

But even that is not enough. You yourself need to get realistic and think through how to break up your own IT project into pieces that are digestible. Yes, you. You need to study the situation to a level of detail where you have a good grip on the various moving parts, and how the project can get teased apart, like undoing a tangled knot. Think it through from beginning to end and from top to bottom, whiteboard it with colleagues, make notes, do some research, discuss it with many different advisors of different types, and above all be very skeptical when someone tells you any aspect of it is going to be easy. Remember, the devil is in the details, and nothing is simple. That being said, don't get lost in the weeds. You need to stay at the functional area / software module level, not the feature level. To put this in Agile terminology, you want to stay at the initiative and epic level and refrain from delving down into user stories and tasks.

You can hire a big-name IT consulting firm and they may assign their best people, or their worst. Ask for bios, read the bios, and interview the consultants they are trying to park at your organization for extended engagements. Interview them as if they were permanent hires. Only engage a firm that is right sized for your organization. A large multi-national firm will deploy their top consultants to their largest most important clients, not to you; and vice-versa, if your organization is very large, then a tiny boutique consultancy with sixteen employees will not be able to handle your project. A clue that might tip you off that the prospective consulting firm is too small is if their CEO shows up at your office to personally conduct the demo and then tells you that their proprietary intellectual property add-on module will get migrated to the latest operating system as soon as "the" programmer gets back from his vacation. This actually happened to one of our clients. By the way, that project failed to deliver on its promises in the expected timeframe and suffered many years of delays.

Now that you have followed the first two Core Concepts, **Embrace Change** and **Seek Balance**, you are finally prepared to begin the project in earnest. You have examined your policies, you have cleansed your data, you have championed change, you have hired the right people, you have a realistic doable phased scope on the drawing board. That's great news; however, at this juncture, you can still fail.

Here is where you need to gain the wisdom contained in our third Core Concept, **Act as One**. In the next three Core Concept Components, you are going to learn how to staff the project (**Free Our People**), how to take effective action and design the new system (**Meet to Act**), and how to keep track of the progress and keep the project on track (**Write to Read**). Here are the remaining three critical strategic principles that you must absorb. We present them in a straightforward and direct manner.

We are imparting to you the wisdom gained from suffering. We have suffered through too many wasted efforts. The great shame of it is how unnecessary all of it was. By following the concepts presented in this book, you can save your organization from wasting millions of dollars and years of futile toil. The extent of the waste is enormous, as is the extent of the opportunity we have now to understand why IT systems implementations go sideways, and how to stay on the right road. You too can prosper by joining The Zen of IT revolution.

CHAPTER 7

Free Our People

The Master was growing old, so one day the monks hid his gardening tools, thinking that he should not have to work anymore.

The Master, unable to find his tools, immediately understood what had happened and said that he would stop eating until his tools were returned.

The monks quickly returned the tools, and the Master returned to the field saying, "A day of no work is a day of no eating."

Free Our People

A new software is selected at the culmination of a software selection project from a short list of leading contenders. The new software is selected along with a consulting company that is needed to implement it. The cost of putting in the new system is mostly the cost of paying the consultants to implement it. Yes, the license costs for the software itself are hefty, nowadays being monthly subscription fees per named user, but the cost of the consultants will surpass the cost of the software, at least in the first year, and especially if there are over-runs. The implementers send in their consultants and those consultants figure out how to meet the existing business requirements using the new, different, and better software, or perhaps using an up-to-date version of the legacy software (which has changed so much that, for all intents and purposes, it is a new app).

The solution of how to meet the existing requirements with the new software takes place first in the analysis phase, and later on, in much more detail during the design phase. On smaller projects the analysis (high level) phase and the design phase (detail level) are merged into a single phase. We are talking about implementation methodology phases, not project scope phases. On very small projects, the consultants simply train the users on the new software, do a quick and dirty data conversion by importing lists of customers, vendors, and the like from Excel templates, and then just bring the system live, ironing out the kinks in production. Obviously, that simplistic approach is insufficient for any IT project of even modest complexity.

The terminology of the implementation phases of an IT project vary with the fashions just like any other IT buzzwords. Simply put, the phases, in chronological order, are discovery (high-level scoping), analysis (requirements gathering), detailed design (solutioning), build (configurations, setups, integrations, application customizations, and custom reporting), system

testing, application deployment, user training, data conversion, user acceptance testing (UAT), final cut-over, go live, and post implementation support. These phases need to be done, no matter what buzzwords you give them
or what kind of fancy methodology you claim to have. Pure and simple, you
need to do all this stuff before you can stand up a new system or even part of
a new system such as one functional area or software module. In other words,
if you are phasing the project in by module and doing the General Ledger as
a first step, you need to do ALL these implementation steps for just that one
project phase. Simply put, for each project phase you must complete every
implementation phase.

The Players

Consultants are either technical or functional. Technical consultants are programmers and systems or software engineers, whereas functional consultants
are application experts. Technical consultants know computer languages,
networks, and hardware whereas functional consultants know how to configure, set up and use the application being implemented. Some functional
consultants also know the technical side of things as well and can even do
custom programming. The consulting-side business analysis is performed by
the functional consultants (application specialists) in most cases. Now hear
this: consultants cannot successfully implement an IT project, unless all the
other players do their part, and all these core concepts are taken to heart and
put to good use. To successfully stand up a new IT system, consultants must
work in a healthy, cooperative, positive, change-friendly environment, not a
toxic political warzone.

Managers are people who have vague notions about magical improvements but do not understand how the legacy system works at any level of
detail. Managers aren't supposed to know those details; they are supposed to
understand the high-level goals and lead their team. Managers must be the
champions of change. Managers must participate in the change management

promotional campaign. Without their active and passionate support, the project will flounder. The leadership abilities of managers are crucial for success.

End-users are people who understand the legacy system at the very deepest levels of minutia; however, they understand only their tiny little cog in a
very immense wheel. They are given the title of subject matter experts and
indeed they are the true experts. You must talk directly to the end-users to
have a true understanding of what is going on. Many end-users will have had
no experience being part of the implementation of a new IT system because
they have been using the same antiquated system for their entire career at
their company.

Business Analysts are hired by companies to act as translators and liai-
sons between the computer nerds and the end-users (many of whom are in
clerical roles that involve a lot of data entry). Business analysts know how to
capture a comprehensive list of process steps and create Visio diagrams that
document the current state, whereas most users are not good at doing this
themselves, because it's not what they do on a daily basis. Client-side business analysts are a luxury that many IT projects do not have the budget for. It
will be worthwhile for your organization to hire some if you don't have them
already before undertaking a sizable IT project.

Project Managers can be internal (client-side) or external (consulting-side). Project managers list and track the tasks of the project, including
due dates using project management software. They often do not understand
enough about the work being performed to gauge whether the project is actually on track or woefully behind schedule; good project managers are able
to identify who on the project does know the truth about the real status of
the project and they rely upon those experts to get a clear reading, and they
are fearless about dealing with the realities, instead of engaging in wishful
thinking. Good project management is, like change management, completely essential, and not merely a nice-to-have. Any complex IT project must
have project management talent. Ideally, there should be a client-side project

manager and a consulting-side project manager. The two project managers then form a check-and-balance partnership which keeps everybody honest.

If you do not have internal project management onboard and are going to rely completely on the consulting firm to manage your large-scale IT project, because you think it's too expensive to hire your own client-side project management, then beware that without the checks and balances and scrutiny, this lack of oversight may end up costing you much more than the compensation for the new client-side project manager would have been, as you are at risk of being over-charged by the consultants. Hire a project manager if you need to. The project manager in almost all cases nowadays will follow a Lean and/or Agile project management methodology. Lean and Agile is better than traditional waterfall methodology and will help your project succeed; however, as we discussed at length in the previous Core Concept Component, **Manage Our Miracle**, it is not in and of itself the solution, nor the most important key to success.

The Roles

It is important that every stakeholder participates in the project, but it is essential that you array a ton of top IT talent on the project. You will not win the game unless your team has great players. Yes, you must have great coaching and the support of loyal fans, but you cannot win using fans (users) and coaches (project managers), you need the actual players (highly skilled and very technical IT professionals). These IT professionals are functional application experts and technical experts in networking, databases, data warehousing, business intelligence reporting and dashboards, custom programming, on-going data integrations and interfaces, and one-time data conversions (also called data migrations). You must have good skilled resources in all these IT functional and technical areas, and you have to vet them yourself. You cannot rely on any consulting firm to send you the good eggs. They may send you rotten eggs and charge you the same high hourly rate. You must remain skeptical until you see good results. Gauging results is discussed in our final Core Concept Component, **Write to Read**. If the consultants do not appear to know what the heck they are doing, it is probably because they don't.

IT systems designers are implementers who have functional skills (they know the apps) and/or technical skills (they know computer programming). This kind of talent isn't what you think it is. Most people who are staffing IT projects with IT talent get this very wrong. They think that they are implementing an app or perhaps implementing a technology platform, but that is wrong; they are designing a new part of an IT system within a living breathing IT ecosystem. It doesn't matter what particular brand of app you are implementing. This is a shocker. For example, most people think that if they are implementing a particular ERP, such as Dynamics 365 Finance, or a CRM such as Salesforce, or a reporting system, such as Tableau, the best person for the job is always somebody who has spent his or her entire career focused on that particular application. This is false.

For example, a good house painter can use Benjamin Moore paints, or Sherwin-Williams paints. It doesn't really matter. A good taxicab driver could drive a Ford or a Toyota. It doesn't really matter. What matters is if the person can conduct a proper business analysis, come up with creative solutions, document their design clearly, get along well with collaborators, and whether they have relevant industry experience, knowledge of programming in general, knowledge of accounting in general, knowledge of business functional areas in general, and whether they are conscientious, meticulous, reliable, and have good references. Unfortunately, too many times, these truly important attributes are not the focus of the IT talent search. Much too much emphasis is placed on finding candidates whose entire careers are focused on that one particular app, and in cases where that app is a hot product (which it usually is because that's probably why you selected it) the recruiters are narrowing the candidate pool down to a point where you end up with the few bad apples that don't have a job because they are incompetent. Sadly, all that seems to matter to hiring managers is how many years that person has worked with that particular brand application. This is myopic to say the least.

Too often the IT talent search is constrained to people who have memorized every menu navigation option in one single app. So what? They know every menu in an app. So what? They worked on only one app their entire life. So what? They may not know anything more than where stuff is in one app. You need to vet them as far as all the truly important attributes mentioned above. A smart, creative, analytical person who is a great designer and skilled at documentation, can work on just about any IT system and learn it as they go along. You need to find well-rounded creative individuals with broad skill sets, not menu monkeys and feature freaks.

Everyone involved in the project should stick to their role and their assigned role must be something that they are good at and that they actually know how to do properly. Project managers should not stray into business analysis and start trying to design the system (unless they are also experts in system design, which is most often not the case). Users should not be given ANY homework beyond being interviewed, critiquing the iterative prototypes, and testing the system when it's ready for user acceptance testing. In all likelihood, they won't do their homework (because they won't have time or won't even know how to do it) and the project will stall.

Top management such as C-Level officers should participate at an appropriately high level and not get lost in the weeds or be required to approve decisions when in reality they have no time to spend reviewing the feature or user-interface options. They will become a bottleneck. The C-Levels should mostly be there to enforce the adoption of the system by being very visible and very insistent that the new system is going into production come hell or high water. This may be all they need to do, but it is a crucial role. They play the scary boss and/or the pumped-up cheerleader and they wake users up to the reality that this is truly going happen this time; we are all going onto a new system, and it's going to be a good thing for everyone. Enforcing adoption through an artful balance of enthusiasm and threat is a very necessary component that is usually missing on IT system implementations. This lack of executive presence and executive enforcement is because top executives are political animals that are often best at shielding themselves from risk and hedging their bets. They shouldn't be allowed to play those games. They need to get in everybody's face and put their own neck on the chopping block as well.

Users should participate by being interviewed by the IT systems implementers and/or business analysts, taking part in collaborative iterative prototyping, and then testing the system when it's time to do so. That's pretty much it. Giving them anything else to do is usually a mistake. They should not be given a lot of "homework" in the form of creating coding schemes, cleansing data, preparing data conversions, analyzing, and commenting on design documents, and so forth. They don't have time and they won't do it very well even if they do find the time. The work will be delivered late and will be flawed, and typically will have to be redone by an IT consultant (internal or external).

For example, they will create alpha codes with lead zeros such as 001, 002, 003, instead of 100, 110, 120 (avoiding lead zeros and leaving space between the numbers). A programmer knows that Excel will chop off the lead zeros and knows to leave space in numerical sequence codes. Users design sequence codes of only five digits, whereas a programmer knows that seven or more digits will ensure the numbers don't turn over. These are just two small examples of the hundreds of different kinds of mistakes they will make due to a lack of experience.

Also, when discussing the feasibility of features and capabilities a programmer is framing things in terms of how the information is stored and organized (or perhaps missing from) a database. Users think only in terms of the screens of the application. The computer system to them is a screen with data on it. To a programmer the screen is the least of what they think about it; programmers think about data, where it is, how much there is, how to accumulate it, the relationships between the various data sets, how to join information together, and so forth. Without having an appreciation of (nor an understanding of) how to programmatically manipulate data, what an end-user is able to contribute to the design of a computer system is severely limited.

Furthermore, users won't ever read design documents. A proper design document is a blueprint which can be used as a build order and covers a functional area and/or application module, and it specifies the intricate detail of the setup and configuration. Surely you must be dreaming if you expect users to actually read and provide detailed written feedback on a fifty-page technical document. Because they won't read it, does not mean that you shouldn't write it. We will go over the topic of documentation in the last Core Concept Component, **Write to Read**. For now, simply realize and fully appreciate the limited capacity and ability of the users to contribute meaningfully on an IT project with regard to design.

Users are invaluable and irreplaceable in their three primary roles: subject matter experts who are interviewed so that the designer can understand the as-is process, reviewers who provide iterative feedback on the design as it unfolds, and testers who participate in user acceptance testing. Don't expect clerical application end-users to do much beyond that on the project. They aren't good at what they don't do for a living. End-users are intelligent hard-working people who usually know more about the intricacies of the business processes than their bosses do, or the IT consultants will ever know. But they don't design and build computer systems for a living. You wouldn't expect Jimi Hendrix to design or build the electronic circuitry in a Marshall guitar amplifier or a fuzz box. You wouldn't expect Andre Segovia to chop down a tree and construct a guitar out of it. You wouldn't expect Glenn Gould or Billy Joel to design and build a Steinway grand piano.

You won't save money by having tasks that should be assigned to a technical IT expert (which are chargeable by the hour at high rates) done by your salaried employees (for free in essence because they are already on the payroll), because your salaried employees don't know how to do those tasks properly and they won't have the time to do them anyway. If you rely on users to do analysis, design, and build work you will delay your IT project, often to the point of project failure.

Every organization has several important employees who are experts in many facets of the business. Sometimes they are folks that were in a clerical role who have worked their way up to managerial levels. These people know the business inside and out and they may have worked at the organization for decades, wearing many hats and serving in many capacities over the years. Some of these folks are workaholics and need to learn about work/life balance, but in any case, they are invaluable resources. They may be new or recent hires, but they have a long history in their industry and may know more than anybody in the company about what needs to be done. These folks are the best subject matter experts in the organization. You can't do an IT project without good subject matter experts because without them you would have absolutely no idea what to do. These types of super subject matter experts can not only tell you what is going in the trenches, but they understand the inner workings of the organization including interactions with customers, vendors, suppliers, banks, governmental agencies, and the general public, as well as strategy and the future direction of the industry and the organization. The pain-points they reveal and the wish-lists they come up with are essential guideposts on the design journey.

If your organization is planning to embark upon a large-scale IT systems implementation project, one of the smartest things you can do is to free up one or more of these super subject matter experts from their day-to-day responsibilities. If the subject matter expert is not freed from their day-to-day operational responsibilities, then those day-to-day responsibilities will always come first. If a customer needs something or a quarterly report needs to be submitted to the government, they will cancel their IT project meeting in a heartbeat. This means that a very key member (or members) of the IT project team will not be available to contribute much; the project will bog down, and probably fail. These key people who understand most of the inner workings of the organization and your industry must be freed up to focus 100% on the IT project. The idea that they will spend 40% of their time on the project and 60% of their time on operations is a fallacy. If operations is even 1% of their job, it will become 100%. Their job description needs to be re-written entirely; they need a new job title. They must be completely dedicated to the project, otherwise, you can consider them just another end-user.

Obviously, you cannot free up all your users from operations. As stated above, users should have very minimal responsibility for the project, because they won't have time and they won't be able to focus, and most of them only understand their limited role. However, a large-scale IT implementation requires seriously good subject matter experts (at least one, and maybe more if possible, and maybe different ones in different areas and disciplines). You can consider these special subject matter experts to be super-users who are trained in the new software and become the new trainer, in a train-the-trainer approach. You can consider them as internal consultants. Sometimes these people are new hires who were formerly implementation consultants themselves and, in those cases, thinking of them as internal consultants is very fitting. You have a choice; either hire an internal consultant or hire a new operations person who can back fill as you transfer your operational expert out of operations and offer them a new job as a 100% focused resource on the IT project. Depending on the size of your organization and the extent of your digital transformation initiative, you may need to do this with several roles.

When key subject matter experts are not freed up from operational responsibility this becomes another major reason for IT project failure. They are asked to devote a percentage of their time to the project, but this is ridiculous because they already work forty or sometimes sixty or seventy hours a week and are heavily overloaded with operational duties. The most knowledgeable and gung-ho among your employees are the workaholics who typically take on more operational responsibilities than anyone else and work longer hours. Where are these extra hours for new system design supposed to come from?

If you are trying to pull off some immense digital transformation initiative within your organization to shepherd your users out of the 1980s and into the new world of cloud-computing, big data, the internet of things, and artificially intelligent Agile workstreams, but you are doing this without first making sure that you have at least one employee that is totally focused on this initiative, you are being unrealistic. Having said that, please understand that the heavy lifting will be done by highly skilled IT professionals. Top management, IT project managers, super-user subject matter experts, and clerical users all have important roles to play, and if any of these folks neglect their duties or confuse their role, the project suffers. You must have all the ingredients and mix them together at the right time in the right way. But it's most important to understand what is typically lacking so that you will not make the typical mistakes.

Typically lacking from a staffing perspective, in order of importance, is the following:

- Enough technical IT talent that has been vetted
- Super-user subject matter experts who have been freed 100% from day-to-day operations
- High-level managers such as VP's and C-Levels enforcing change, cheerleading, and putting their own head on the chopping block (instead of keeping their distance and setting up scapegoats)

- Client-side project management (relying on the consulting firm to manage the project by themselves; can someone say, "Overcharge me, please"?)

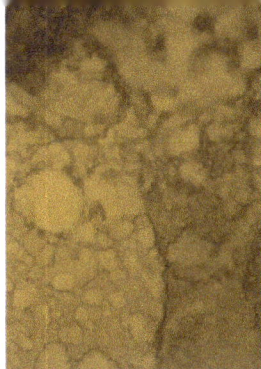

CHAPTER 8

Meet to Act

Two monks were arguing about a flag.

One said, "The flag is moving."

The other said, "The wind is moving."

The Master happened to be walking by and said, "It is not the flag that moves; it is not the wind that moves. It is the mind that moves."

Meet to Act

Project meetings are of vital importance because that is where the design happens. No design, no build, no system. A designer cannot design without decisions and agreements from the management and input from the users on many aspects of the design. Project meetings are also the main source of information on the current state and for understanding the workings of the legacy system (i.e., the as-is study).

How often to meet, who should attend, who should moderate, and how feedback, decisions, statuses, outcomes, and next steps should be logged and communicated is largely the heart of the Agile project management methodology. Discussing the ins and outs of the various Agile ceremonies is not of the purpose of this book. We urge you to get Agile training, read articles and books on the subject, and follow the Agile project management methodology as adopted by your organization and/or the consulting firm you have engaged for your IT project. The Agile approach is a vast improvement over the traditional waterfall approach. Take advantage of that.

We warn you against thinking that if you label all your meetings with Agile terminology, you are indeed being agile, nimble, or efficient. The same tedious pointless meetings may be occurring under an Agile framework banner as were occurring in the waterfall days. Furthermore, we strongly warn you against becoming so entranced and hypnotized by the promise of Agile and the compulsion to feel current, hip, acceptable, and relevant that your primary focus becomes the appearance that you are adhering and in-the-know of Agile principles and buzzwords. Your primary focus should be getting your outdated, spaghetti code systems replaced with modern, efficient, cloud-based applications that may start out with bare bones functionality, but can serve as a platform on which to build, adding features such as automated data integrations, user-friendly interdepartmental workflows, artificial intelligence, paperless technology (to name a few) through continuous process improvement. Such a modern IT system will allow your organization to thrive in the coming decades freed of the hindrance of outmoded archaic technology.

Meetings, Meetings, and more Meetings

Even though you may find yourself attending an "Agile" meeting, you are still in a meeting. And bad things happen in meetings, be they agile meetings or less than agile meetings. If you don't know how to avoid what typically goes wrong inside IT systems design meetings you have a big problem. This chapter exposes what really happens in these meetings and why so many of them are inefficient, counter-productive, boring, frustrating, and often a grand waste of time. These meetings are usually attended by a combination of project managers, software engineers, business managers, and end-users.

We have attended many thousands of IT systems design meetings over the last thirty years. We have seen the good, the bad, and the ugly. The primary problem with IT systems design meetings is that the participants fail to think systematically and methodically but instead think episodically and anecdotally. To explain what we mean by this, we will use an analogy. Pretend that you are an alien from a distant solar system (an IT consultant) and you are conducting a meeting with earthlings (your client) to learn about the Earth (the cash management process at a manufacturing company). You know nothing about the Earth. A good line of questioning starts at the highest level and systematically covers all the major topics which comprise the area of study, culminating in a logical outline, the details of which are to be filled in later during subsequent meetings.

A good line of questioning for our alien visiting the Earth to pose might go something like this:
- Does your planet have oceans or is it all land?

- Okay, you have oceans, is the land one mass of land or broken into continents?
- Okay, how many continents do you have and are they approximately the same size?
- Good, there are only seven of them. What are the names of the continents?
- And so on…

As consultants we are often lectured by consulting directors and salespersons that we should let the client speak for as long as they want to. Never interrupt the client; we are reminded. Really listen to what the client (i.e., operational manager or application end-user) has to say and take it all in, we are chided. But that approach is dead wrong. We must not let the client babble on and on. As an IT systems designer (often referred to as a solutions architect) you must interrupt the client constantly. Most clients do not know how to think in terms of IT system design, because they don't design IT systems for a living. Listening to them talk and take the conversation into a cul-de-sac or a wild tangent as they chase after every red herring that pops into their brain is a waste of time that we can ill afford. Rather than let them spew forth their diatribes which typically are much too granular and resemble griping and venting sessions more than systematic descriptions of their functional area, their responses should be limited to directly answering the laser-focused questions posed to them by a knowledgeable, experienced, and talented IT systems solution architect. A professional IT system designer must guide the conversation with a line of logical questioning, and keep gently (or if need be, not so gently), prodding the client (manager or end-user) back into the logical line of questioning, because they will invariably stray off the path.

Back to our analogy, our last question was what are the names of the continents? Here is where the interviewee starts to waste time. He will mention Antarctica and he will complain about how cold it is there and what a pest the penguins are. Then he will go into extreme detail about how the penguins sit for extended periods of time warming and guarding their eggs and all the trials and tribulations of the beleaguered penguins. The designer patiently listens to the client describe in excruciating detail numerous aspects of penguins including their mating rituals. Then what happens is the meeting ends because you run out of time. You never got the names of Australia, Europe, or Asia. You don't have an outline. You don't have a high-level overview. You don't know what you are dealing with in totality. You know a lot about penguins, but you don't know that there more than a billion people living in China and another billion plus in India. You have a collection of useless detailed anecdotes and minutia that may be jotted down in Microsoft Word or OneNote or scribbled on a whiteboard, or more likely simply dissipated into the air like cigarette smoke and lost forever. That "information" will never amount to anything. The client got to talk for two solid hours. Whoopie!

This seems like a silly joke and seems like it's common sense and you may wonder how this could be a problem. Nonetheless, THIS IS EXACTLY THE REAL PROBLEM WITH MEETINGS. Most IT system design meetings are a waste of time because there is no enforcement of an intelligent focused line of questioning which goes from top to bottom, starts with a high-level outline, and logically progresses to a sequence of subsequent meetings in which the details for the various parts are captured, documented, and understood IN A LOGICAL ORDER of slowly increasing granularity.

People tend to drill down into the minutia as soon as any topic is brought up. It is the natural tendency of the human mind to follow a train of thought as if you are clinking hyperlinks on YouTube. You may have started out looking for a how-to video which provides instructions for resetting the tire pressure indicator in your Honda Accord and end up watching a documentary on Egyptian pyramids replete with shocking news about the age of the Sphinx. In these meetings, politeness and tact dictate that we allow the subject matter expert to talk about their job responsibilities without any guidance or interruption. Although our politeness may avoid hurting any-body's feelings, or wounding anybody's pride, or ruffling anybody's feathers, no valuable work will be accomplished. It is assumed that "the project is getting done" because we held a meeting and the subject matter expert talked about their functional area. This is wrong. The project is not getting done, and the meeting was a TOTAL WASTE OF TIME.

Sadly, the typical IT systems design meeting is not an intelligent, system-atic, thorough, and methodical line of questioning, instead it is a freeform conversation. It is a bunch of folks having a "convo". The subject matter experts are clerical users who haven't the foggiest notion about what to talk about in an IT design meeting. They have been doing their same job for twenty years and they have twenty years' worth of useless details to expound upon for umpteen hours. They can ramble on endlessly. These subject matter experts drone on and on as participants fall asleep, turn off their video on the Zoom or Microsoft Teams call, and then mute their audio. They are getting paid but doing nothing (other than surfing the internet on their dual mon-itor or perhaps cooking scrambled eggs or talking to their dog). Nobody is taking notes.

The conference call meeting is being recorded (no need to take notes, right?). However, nobody will ever watch or listen to that recording. Nothing whatsoever has been accomplished. These conversations (which are not true IT system design meetings) will go on for several months. At the end of this time span there will be lots of useless meetings recorded and a status field in the project management software which ticks off the boxes showing that the meetings did indeed happen as planned in accordance with the Agile proj-ect management methodology. The methodology is being followed (or so it is thought). However, no IT system is being designed. All that is happen-ing is that people are getting on conference calls, having conversations, and randomly talking about the minutia of various persnickety business issues, arcane one-off problems, intricate transactional details, wish-list possibilities, pain-point headaches, potential solutions, as-is process descriptions, and the history of how the system evolved into the current mess that it is in. There is no point in having all these conversations because there are no outcomes, no decisions, no concrete results, and nothing is gained by it. It is a grand waste of time.

The project will never get done until an IT systems designer who knows what he or she is doing takes over. The IT systems designer must have force of authority, strength of character and plenty of charisma to lead and focus the conversation and construct a useful outline of topics. After the outline of topics is constructed, the designer should systematically add details at the right level of granularity for each topic, one-by-one in order, without getting lost in weeds, and without leaving out any topic. The results should then be written up in a design document which is the evidence that something is actually being accomplished.

Often the takeaways from a meeting are sloppily jotted on a whiteboard during the meeting. It is essential that somebody takes the time to translate the rough-hewn whiteboard notes into clear, concise, prose. Rarely does this happen because everyone is exhausted, drained, and mostly sleepy from the meeting, and they just want to go home. Writing up the results of the meetings takes discipline which is often lacking. Nobody enforces this. It is generally considered enough of an accomplishment that you showed up at the meeting and that's it. Even if you took no notes and said absolutely nothing, you did your so-called work. Furthermore, if the meeting was a scattered conversation, rather than a logical line of questioning, there is really no point in writing it up anyway.

A farmer plows a field for a purpose. The goal is food. You don't just play around in the dirt and expect to get delicious corn on the cob. You systematically plow in straight lines, then the next step is sowing seeds, then you must add fertilizer, and so on. Something good comes out of the mud because you followed a systematic approach. In order for anything good to come out of

IT systems design meetings, you must also follow a systematic approach. The IT systems design is not going to just magically appear. The evidence of your labor in the corn field is edible corn. The evidence of your labor in IT systems design meetings is a write-up of the design which may or may not also include a mock-up and/or a working prototype app.

Documentation and prototyping is the subject of our last Core Concept Component, **Write to Read**, and we will delve into that topic next. However, the subject of meetings and the subject of documentation, mock-ups and prototypes are closely related. Here is the unfortunate mistake that we have seen repeated by so many, and so many times, that it truly makes us sad: the status of an IT systems project is gauged by the project manager based on task completion or percentage of completion of tasks, and tasks are marked as complete or partially complete when a meeting is held, attended, and concluded. A meeting is defined as a task. The mistake is in thinking that the fact that the meeting actually occurred, and that people actually bothered to sit through it (even though they may have been nodding off), is in of itself representative of progress on the project. Thankfully, the fallacy that a meeting is a task is being abolished by the Lean and Agile project management methodology. Milestones should be deliverables, not merely that a meeting was conducted.

When you are building a house, the progress can be easily seen. Is there a foundation? Are there walls? Is there a roof? Has the sewer line been hooked up? Is the electricity turned on? Has the hardwood floor been installed? Has the exterior been painted? Has the interior been painted? Is the HVAC system operational? Walls, a roof, flooring, paint, carpets, a furnace, running water, and a paved driveway provide concrete evidence and irrefutable proof that the house is indeed getting built. An inspector or construction project manager can walk through the building site and literally see the progress with his or her own two eyes. Not so, when you are building an IT system.

You can't see any large concrete solid three dimensional objects. The whole thing is hidden in streams of zeros and ones and a dizzying array of randomly named Excel and Word files scattered haphazardly on a SharePoint site or worse yet, trapped in Outlook Email chains. You can't see it; hence, you may not realize that it's all useless rubbish which will eventually be scrapped.

You see people sitting in conference rooms. You see people attending meetings. You see whiteboards filled with scribbling. You look at project status reports where the list of scheduled design meetings has been duly checked off. The meetings were scheduled. The participants attended all of them at the scheduled time. You smile happily and believe the IT systems project is getting done, but you are terribly mistaken. Yes, the meetings are happening. So what? The meetings are all a grand waste of time, and NOTHING IS DONE! You cannot believe that nothing is getting done. What about all those meetings? What about the meetings attended by consultants that are charging your organization two hundred dollars per hour or more? You believe that because you are spending a lot of money, surely you must be getting a lot of results, right? WRONG.

To know that an IT systems project is actually getting done there must be some concrete and irrefutable EVIDENCE. Unfortunately, what constitutes evidence is not so obvious to most people, even so-called IT project managers. It should be obvious, but unbelievably it is not. Meetings are NEVER evidence of any kind of progress. The number of meetings and the number of people who attend those meetings and the frequency of those meetings are not a gauge of progress, nor evidence of making headway. When it comes to IT system design, there are only three types of valid evidence: peer reviewed design artifacts, screen mock-ups reviewed by managers and users, and critiqued working prototype applications. We delve further into the subject of evidence for progress on IT systems implementations in the next chapter, **Write to Read**.

Decisions, Decisions, Decisions...

Now let us turn our attention to another major problem with meetings. Nobody wants to make decisions about anything. People are gun shy about finalizing any decision because they don't want to have to strain their brain to think it all the way through, or else they don't want to be blamed in the future for a stupid decision they made today. They delay every decision with the result that the meeting accomplishes nothing.

As an analogy, imagine you are in a restaurant. The waiter comes to your table and asks if you have decided what you would like to eat. It is perfectly reasonable to ask questions about whether the fish is farmed or wild caught, whether a baked potato is included with the entrée, and whether or not you can substitute rice pilaf for broccoli. However, it is not okay to keep telling the waiter you need more time and to come back later, over and over again, more than a dozen times, until the restaurant closes and everybody at your table goes home hungry. Yet this is exactly what happens in IT system design meetings. The decision makers are managers and end-users. They are fond of saying something like this, "we can decide on that later" or "we'll figure that out later" or "we'll set that up when the time comes."

The old adages "there's no time like the present" and "never put off till tomorrow what you can do today" are very apropos here. A perfect example is numbering or ID schemes such as sales order number, invoice number, purchase order number, customer ID, vendor ID, employee ID, inventory item number, and so forth. The truth is that it matters very little what convention you use for ID's other than having enough digits on a sequence to account for future growth. The system will enforce the uniqueness. As a rule of thumb, you should not place a lot of meaning in the ID, but instead have other fields that contain information, but this is not a hard and fast rule. Sometimes it's nice to see the ID and immediately be able to know things from it. For example, all vendors that are domestic could have an ID prefix that begins with DOM and those that are international can begin with INT, and then the sequence can be alpha or numeric, and so forth. Other considerations include whether the ID's can be autogenerated by the system or keyed in by a user or imported from a source system via data integration. There are a lot of different ways to set up numbering schemes. There are innumerable choices for many other types of IT system related decisions all of which may be perfectly valid. ID numbering schemes are just one small example of the kind of decisions we are talking about of which there are literally hundreds if not thousands to be made in the course of designing an IT system.

The bottom line is that most of your IT related decisions simply come down to personal taste. This is not understood. Most people think that all IT related decisions must be a matter of choosing the optimal scientifically and financially correct choice. After all, this is computer science, not computer art, not computer cuisine. The assumption is that IT systems design choices must always be based upon logical choices that must be analyzed scientifically to maximize profits and enhance stakeholder benefits. But the truth is that most of these IT design decisions are nothing other than personal preference. Do you like vanilla, chocolate, or strawberry ice-cream? Should you paint your bathroom blue or green? Should you put pepperoni or sausage on your pizza? It's up to you. It doesn't matter, JUST MAKE A DAMN DECISION!

In IT system design meetings, those with the authority to make decisions, are asked to make some moderately complex decisions which may require cost/benefit analysis, deep thought, or discussion with their peers. Examples of such questions might be as follows: Are you going to print paper disbursement checks or pay your vendors with ACH electronic funds transfers? Are you going to mail paper invoices to customers or mass email invoices as Adobe PDF attachments? Are you going to continue to run that small division which is only 10% of your revenue using the custom MS-Access database application or are we going to include that division as a new department in the new ERP system? Even in these cases where there may be some financial or other measurable impact to the organization, the implications of these decisions are immaterial much of the time. Whatever money you think you might be saving by taking option A instead of option B is nothing compared with how much money you are losing by delaying the IT project due to your indecisiveness.

Yes, even these kinds of moderately complex decisions are of no great importance. In truth, most decisions matter very little. However, what does matter a great deal is that some decision (regardless of what it is) must be made, and made promptly, or the project is going to stall. The delaying of decisions, many of which are merely a matter of personal preference, is a major factor in failed IT system implementations. Agile methodology calls for delaying decisions for as long as possible to wait for maximum information to be gathered, and response to the very latest market conditions, abiding by a just-in-time mentality. This may be true when coding commercial software but is not true in implementing off-the-shelf or cloud SaaS applications. Most organizations do not develop commercial software as their core business, but rather, they license software written by some other company and try to use it to good effect within their organization, and when doing so, they need to make decisions quickly or they will delay the software implementation.

For some weird reason people think that the work of an IT system design meeting does not include the making of firm decisions. Perhaps they believe in some magical parallel reality in which these decisions get made in a nebulous future time that has no correlation with the timetable of the project or of planet Earth. They don't understand that the purpose of the IT systems design meeting is PRECISELY to make all these tedious little personal preference decisions so that the system design can be written up and the work can proceed.

Contrary to Popular Belief, Design is Not a Group Sport

Design is not communal; design is solitary; approval and tweaking of the design can be communal. Paul McCartney and John Lennon didn't sit in a room with George Harrison, Ringo Starr, and George Martin to write songs as a group activity. Paul went off on his own and John and George likewise went off on their own, and eventually they each came up with their own separate songs. That solitary process often took longer than the time spent in the recording studio. They presented a song to the group by singing it as they strummed a guitar or banged on a piano. Feedback was provided. The song was tweaked. A decision was made as to whether to bother to try to record it. We think that we can design IT systems as a group activity but doing so is terribly inefficient and most often a futile endeavor. Even if we reduce the number of participants to five people as Agile principles suggest and which is a very good idea, the actual design work should nonetheless be solitary or perhaps involve no more than two or three people.

We know of a case where a long meeting was attended by seventeen people including the COO, the Director of IT, along with several programmers, departmental managers, and end-users. This meeting consisted of nothing more than a tedious and preposterous discussion about what the values should be in one dropdown box in one field of an HR application. We never managed to get to the second field in the tab order. This one field took three hours. At the conclusion of the meeting nothing was decided regarding what values should go in the dropdown box. The group did, however, make one decision. They decided to meet again in three weeks. Three weeks later the same pointless conversation ate up another three hours of everyone's life, and you guessed it, the only decision that came out of it was to meet again, this time in five weeks instead of three, due to the upcoming holidays. The pace of this IT project was glacial. After seven years and millions of dollars spent, they were still running their old inefficient system.

The field they were trying, unsuccessfully, to define was the employee type. Employees have different attributes such as whether they are full-time vs. part-time, international vs. domestic, contractors vs. perm hires, admin vs. billable, and so on. The problem with a single field holding multiple attributes is one that is well understood by experienced computer programmers and database modelers. The answer is to create multiple fields instead of trying to fit everything in one field. For example, you shouldn't have a single field (data element) called "Car" with a dropdown that has a value such as "2022 Red Ford Mustang Convertible with Black Leather Interior." You should have these separate fields: year, color, make, model, and interior trim. End-users don't understand this basic data modeling concept. These discussions are useless and go around in circles and no decision is arrived at. What should happen instead is that a professional IT systems solution architect should interview users and a study of the legacy system should be conducted. Then the solutions architect should go off by his or herself and design tables, fields, module configurations, reports, or what-have-you, and capture the design in technical and function design documents (specs), and perhaps illustrate that design further using a PowerPoint slide deck, Visio diagrams, screen mock-ups, and/or prototype apps during iterative feedback meetings. The design will be tweaked, revamped, rejected, or approved in those iterative feedback sessions which are sometimes referred to as joint application design (JAD) sessions or some other buzzword from the deep well of IT buzzwords. Perhaps the term "JAD session" is now considered an anachronism. Who cares? You know what we mean.

Summary

Rather than holding design meetings with all those involved attending and chiming in, you should have professional IT designers conduct interviews, observe operations, perform research, and then go off and design things by themselves or with a few other designers, and then when they are ready, present those designs in the form of slide decks, design documents, screen mock-ups, and prototypes for review, feedback, and approval to the people who will be using what they have designed. An iterative process of design and feedback can ensue.

What we are saying here doesn't sound like anything revolutionary, new, or profound; however, here we are giving you the straight dope. These problems are precisely what bogs down IT projects. Unstructured design "conversations" are one of the main reasons that IT projects fail. We have seen it too many times to count.

HERE IS THE BLUNT TRUTH:

Not only are your business rules and policies over complicated for no good reason, not only is your data full of duplicate records and bad values, not only have you neglected change management, not only are your C-Levels hiding out in a bunker, not only have you bitten off way more than you can chew with your bloated feature scope which includes every bell and whistle and nice-to-have in creation, not only is your project scope a giant big bang mission impossible which includes every functional area all going live on the same magical day, but to make matters much worse, your design meetings are a waste of time, despite the fact that you have labelled them with Lean and Agile terminology!

Your meetings are pointless exercises in futility because they are random tangential conversations instead of logical lines of questioning, in which nobody makes decisions even when those decisions are simple matters of personal preference, and because you believe that design is a communal affair instead of solitary act that is then presented to the group for approval. Your project manager fails to measure progress using concrete evidence and instead counts off the number of useless meetings that have been attended by bored participants who contributed little of value and absorbed nothing of value.

If your IT project has been going on for nine solid uninterrupted months and your financial burn rate is counted in the tens of thousands, or hundreds of thousands or perhaps even millions of dollars per month, and yet, you cannot point to a small collection of design documents as evidence of progress, then guess what? Your IT project is failing. Another six months, nine months, or two years will not help. Time doesn't create IT systems. Time doesn't help. These aren't trees in the forest that grow by themselves. This isn't Tennessee whiskey in a barrel that is mellowing with age. Time is not your friend here. Time is the enemy. Where is the EVIDENCE OF PROGRESS?

If you phased your project, an evidence of progress might be that you now have a new data staging area where you will be able to perform data migrations and integrations, or you might have a new General Ledger which pulls in the journal entry transactions from the legacy system, or you might have a new CRM and workflow capability which is automating one department as a test pilot, or you might have a collection of completed design documents including technical specifications and functional specifications which have been peer reviewed and signed-off on by department heads, or you might have prototype applications, or a sandbox test environment where you can demonstrate a walkthrough of your most common and basic transactions.

What is baffling is how nobody with any authority notices that a project is in trouble even though there is zero evidence that anything is being accomplished. As long as meetings are being held it is assumed that the project is getting done. If you remember nothing else of this entire Core Concept Component, please remember this: meetings mean absolutely nothing. You must have evidence of progress. If you are not seeing concrete evidence, then fire your consulting firm, hire new people, cancel your contract, reorganize your project, and put somebody else in charge. In other words, DO SOMETHING ABOUT IT.

And if an employee or a contractor points out the fact that there is zero evidence of progress, killing the messenger in the form of removing that pesky whistleblower from the project will not help you in the long run. Yes, it will relieve you of hearing unpleasant news while you still have a job, but when too much time has gone by, and your application is not live, and it is clear to the powers that be that it will never go live, then you will regret that you did not heed the warnings as you work on updating your resume.

You shouldn't need to be warned anyway. As a project manager or steering committee member, you should know enough to look for the evidence and demand the concrete results that show irrefutable progress and prove that your IT project is indeed getting done.

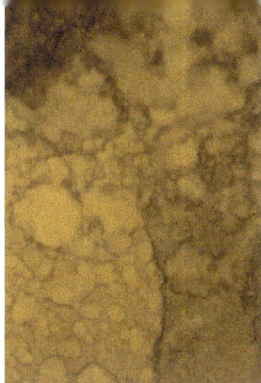

CHAPTER 9

Write to Read

This is the stone,

drenched with rain,

that marks the way.

—*Santōka*

Write to Read

The last Core Concept Component, Write to Read, explains the importance of documentation as it relates to implementing and adopting new or upgraded software for use at your organization. As you may recall from our Core Concept Component, Manage Our Miracle, Agile principle #7 states that **working software is the primary measure of progress**. Furthermore, Agile value #3 states that we should value **working software over comprehensive documentation**.

We agree with the Agile principles, but we are pointing out that these principles were invented by software developers whose daily operations consist of programming and testing their own commercial software code. However, most wasteful IT spending happens at organizations trying to adopt already finished commercial software written by external software vendors. These two situations are very different, and although there is an overlap, different principles are called for in some cases. The vast majority of organizations are not primarily staffed with computer experts. Yes, some organizations do have internal IT talent which does some programming, but most often, if there are customizations required to the base software packages, those customizations will be coded by the software vendor themselves or an implementation partner consulting firm, not by your organization.

When engaged in a large-scale implementation and adoption of new or upgraded software at your organization, the primary measure of progress is **not** working software. The software already works when you buy it, but it is not configured yet, and furthermore you have not decided which features you are going to use, you haven't decided how much of your legacy data to migrate, you haven't trained your users yet, nor even decided how and where to conduct the training. And there are literally thousands of other detailed design and logistical decisions which have yet to be made, most of which just come down to personal preference. And once you make those decisions, guess what? You need to write them down. You can't keep all this information in your head. This is where design documentation comes into play and that is why the primary measure of progress is not working software, but rather, peer-reviewed non-boilerplate functional and technical design artifacts which is how you will record your design decisions.

Peer reviewed means that after the document is written it is published to a forum where at least one fellow IT systems designer reads it word-for-word and provides feedback, including raising a red flag to the project manager if what he or she has just read is useless garbage (as so many of these so-called design documents are). Sadly, we have read more bad design documents in our day, than good ones.

Non-boilerplate means that the so-called design document is something that somebody actually sat down and wrote by themselves and relates directly and specifically to the situation at hand, addressing the unique needs and issues of the client organization. Non-boilerplate IT system design documents are as hard to find as the Holy Grail. To save time, and due to laziness, implementers cut corners by using cut & paste and the "save as" feature of Microsoft Word on the documents from their prior engagements. Most of these so-called design documents are nothing more than a boilerplate template that is sparingly sprinkled with random bits of quasi-information.

Some of these boilerplates are hundreds of pages long and appear quite impressive. However, if you have ever had the displeasure of reading this type of boilerplate tripe, you know that in most cases most sections of the template are not applicable to this particular client and their very unique set of circumstances. Therefore, you wade through page after page of rubbish written by some poor fool who is forced by their employer to adhere to the standards of the template and who was obviously struggling to come up with something (anything) that he or she could quickly jot down into each gaping blank section of the template, even in cases where that section was clearly not applicable.

These badly designed design documents are usually written in Microsoft Word and contain almost exclusively Excel tables (i.e., spreadsheet grids) with very little prose. There is no prose describing the overview, background, context, or explanation of the client or what the client is trying to accomplish. That would require somebody who knows how to write prose and is willing to take the time to explain anything. These documents are loaded with acronyms that are never explained, forming an incomprehensible alphabet soup of rotten ingredients. These Excel grids pasted into Word have too many columns for Word to accommodate even if the document orientation is set to landscape which it usually isn't. What happens is that each column in the grid becomes incredibly narrow to a point where you are reading the contents of each spreadsheet cell one letter at a time. Unbelievably, the author of this rubbish doesn't seem to notice or mind. Perhaps he or she thinks that reading from top to bottom as you might when deciphering ancient Egyptian Hieroglyphic carvings is acceptable, instead of from left to right, as in reading concise intelligible prose written in modern English.

Oftentimes, the search and replace feature (Cntrl-H) is used to replace the prior client name with the current client name, but if the old name is spelled slightly differently throughout the document, you can spot its remnants lurking in certain sections. Nobody has bothered to proofread, because after all, nobody is ever going to read nor make use of any of this garbage anyway. So, what's the point? You can't expect the project manager to actually read any of the documents? Can you? That person just checks them off the list which is more than enough trouble. In effect, the project will be conducted without documentation. The boilerplate is there as window dressing. It is a prop. We can claim to have documentation when in point of fact, there is none.

Proper design document artifacts can be created in Microsoft PowerPoint, Visio, Excel, Word, Adobe PDF, Google Docs, or even as training videos, walkthrough videos or information in Microsoft DevOps, Jira Confluence or other applications used to document your design. These artifacts don't need to be old-school rigid, formal, Microsoft Word templates. That being said, the primary evidence of progress is good design artifacts. Without good design artifacts you cannot build a decent prototype in the sandbox environment, and WITHOUT GOOD DESIGN DOCS YOU WILL NEVER STAND UP YOUR NEW SYSTEM! Lack of good design documentation is a major reason for IT systems implementation failure. We have seen it over and over again.

The realization that we should simplify and streamline IT systems documentation is one of many long-awaited and much needed improvements which Lean and Agile are helping to promote in the IT systems implementation world. However, please don't get confused here, as so many have. Lean and Agile are NOT saying that documentation is no longer important. In fact, it is because documentation is so essential, fundamental, and critical, that we must simplify it and streamline it, and make it less onerous and less formal and constrained.

We need documentation desperately as it is the single most important proof of progress during the discovery, analysis, and the design implementation methodology phases. It is the blueprint to build the new system, and it communicates to all stakeholders the agreed upon approach and scope of each project phase and the feature scope within each phase, as well as explaining the implementation methodology phases you plan to use.

IT systems documents are also referred to as deliverables or artifacts and may include:

- Rapid Assessment Overview / Discovery

- Current State / As-Is Study
- Request for Proposal (RFP)
- Request for Information (RFI)
- IT Systems Proposal / Statement of Work (SOW)
- Project Charter
- Functional Requirements Document (FRD)
- Technical Requirements Document (TRD)
- Solutions Design Document (Functional or Technical or combination)
- Reporting Requirements Document
- Technical Specifications for Integrations, Customizations, Data Conversions, Reports, etc.
- Project Plan
- Cut-over Plan
- Training Manual / User Guide / Job Aid

All these documents are different and serve different purposes. Some of them are more technical and some are more geared toward the layman. Some involve an estimated budget and pricing, some do not. Some strictly limit themselves to what is required by the new system without delving into solutioning. Some of them describe the current system and provide a solution for how to replace and improve it. Sometimes several of the documents can be combined into one big document, especially for smaller-scale IT projects for ease of communication and because the project-size and/or the client-size does not warrant creating multiple documents.

The design IS the design document. Where else does the design exist? Can the design exist in computer programming code, in windows, screens, and command buttons? Theoretically, yes. You can leave out the bothersome and tedious documentation and just "hot dog it," leapfrogging from verbal discussion straight to programming. It's done every day. You can have conversations and start coding an app, then train users how to use it, go live with it, and if something breaks after it goes live, you can reverse engineer the existing code as you try to remember how it works under the hood. You can do that. And in fact, this is done every day in millions of cases and thousands of companies. Some of the quasi-legitimate reasons for leaving out the documentation include understaffed IT departments, extremely time sensitive delivery due dates, and under-funded IT projects. Yes, sometimes there is a valid reason to cut corners, and it is always documentation that is the first thing to get cut (because theoretically, you don't absolutely positively need it).

Do you really need titles and mortgage documents when buying a house? Not really. You could just bring cash to the homeowner and get the keys based on a handshake and a verbal agreement. I mean, you could. Do you really need medical records? Not really. You could just show up at the hospital, a doctor can examine you, hand you a bottle of pills or stitch your up as the case may be, and you could pay cash, or promise to send them a check, and then just walk out. Nothing has to be written down in order for people to do business. But mortgage companies and hospitals never, ever, ever tolerate such slovenly behavior, and in fact, it's against the law for them to do so. However, this kind of reckless disregard for documentation is tolerated in the IT world with the result that many IT projects are harder to do because they start without documentation of the legacy system, and many of these projects fail due to the design not being documented during the design phase.

On IT projects where documentation is not considered important, the design phase goes on for several months (costing a fortune), but it never produces a comprehensive design document. After which, they move into the build phase without a blueprint (a build order). You cannot build a house without a proper architectural blueprint unless you are creating something like a one-room log cabin or an igloo. Why one would think you can stand up a complex IT system without a proper comprehensive write-up of the design is truly baffling, but this goes on all the time. The project fails and is eventually scrapped.

Please take this to heart. There is no design unless there is a design document. The design document may be accompanied by Excel workbooks with long lists of detailed information in spreadsheets that have too many columns to fit legibly on in a page of a Word or PDF file. The document may also be accompanied by screen mock-ups in Microsoft Visio or PowerPoint or some other application. The document may also be accompanied by working prototype applications.

There is no design for a house unless there are plenty of schematics, blueprints, CAD/CAM files, and the like that specify the details of the design in writing. Would a plumber install a toilet, or an electrician repair a fuse box without first writing up a work order that specifies the labor component and what materials are being used? Of course, not. But in IT, we engage in multi-million dollar projects that go on for years without having valid write-ups of what we are doing. We hold meeting, after meeting, after meeting, and no proper design documents ever emerge. Instead, a collection of fragmentary bits of information stored as Excel workbooks, PDF files, PowerPoint slide decks and Word documents begins to fill up an ever-expanding illogical hierarchy of subfolders in SharePoint, Dropbox, OneDrive, or on Google Docs growing like fungus in an abandoned warehouse, until we have a useless morass of disconnected minutia which is worth exactly nothing. No one will ever read it. No one will ever use it.

When the documentation is done right on an IT project, the chance of failure is minuscule. Proper documentation forces the critical issues to be discovered. Proper documentation exposes gaps, clears up misunderstandings, communicates expectations, logs decisions, provides concrete evidence of progress, reveals unrealistic timeframes, and is the blueprint from which the system is configured and the plan from which the deployment is launched. Documentation is so crucial that if you get it wrong you have ZERO CHANCE of success.

The remainder of this Core Concept Component teaches how to get it right when it comes to IT systems documentation.

In an effort to improve documentation standards IT consulting firms as well as internal IT departments launch campaigns aimed at standardizing the documentation process and the documentation artifacts. Usually, these efforts backfire. The well-intentioned folks establishing these documentation standards make two mistakes. Firstly, they require too many types of documents (overcomplicating the process), and secondly, they require designers to strictly adhere to formal and onerous document templates. Because many designs do not really warrant all these different types of documents, and because many designs are for unique one-off situations that could not be foreseen, the poor souls forced to abide by the new documentation standards, struggle to shoehorn their design to fit into the standard document types and templates. They end up with hard to read documents that are mostly blank, because either the entire document or many sections of it don't really apply to the situation at hand.

Why not let the IT systems designer, for whatever it is they are designing, be it custom reports, application customizations, software module setups and configurations, or data integrations, determine (on their own) which types of documents are needed and as well as how to organize each one of them into a logical chapter outline? If the IT designer is capable of designing an IT system (or at least part of one), then wouldn't they also be smart enough and creative enough to come up with a reasonable and sensible way of documenting what they have designed? Why are computer programmers suddenly inept morons who need to be spoon fed documentation boilerplates?

Unfortunately, templates not only don't help, but they make the situation much worse. Overbearing enforcement of document templates are well-meaning attempts at ensuring quality, but in practice they are less than useless, because they are often insulting and burdensome rather than helpful to the IT experts that are forced to use them. For example, if you know how to program a data integration that means that you must already know what sections of information are required, such as data source, data target, direction, timing, error handling, monitoring, notifications, field-by-field mapping, risks, assumptions, batch vs. real-time, and so forth. You don't need a template telling you what a data conversion is all about. If you do, it means that you are not enough of an expert in data integrations to actually create a real one that will work in the real world. It's fine to have a standard template that orders the sections in the same way so as to make all the documentation uniform (especially if there are multiple programmers working on the data integrations at a single client, which in many cases, there aren't), but in actual practice, uniformity of documentation is not all that important. Really, who cares if two well-written, clear, and concise integration design documents have slightly different sections, are ordered slightly differently, and use different fonts and font sizes? What we need is relevant information, not agreement on font sizes and chapter titles.

What is important is that a skilled data integration programmer takes the time to write down (in any format he or she wants) the relevant facts about that data integration. Do they have to write that down in a Word document that follows a precise template? Absolutely not. These templates are a straitjacket to a creative person. It takes a creative person to write computer programs and design IT systems including reports, business process workflows, dashboards, data feeds and the like. These creative folks despise being confined to rigid templates. Would you confine a movie director and screenplay writer to a rigid template of story boards, such as boy meets girl, boy loses girl, and so on? Would you get a masterpiece like Casablanca if you did?

Can the data integration documentation be stored as meta-data inside of the data integration middleware platform itself? Surely it can. You don't need "documents" per se as in Microsoft Word or Adobe PDF files, but you need "documentation" in the form of relevant information that is at an appropriate level of granularity. The information should be detailed enough to provide enough of a breadcrumb trail to make supporting, enhancing, and troubleshooting the integration efficient. The documentation exists only for the purpose of maintenance of the code. Nobody reads this stuff for fun. Nobody is going to read it other than an IT expert who is trying to fix a broken integration.

All of your documentation needs to be reviewed by someone other than the author. At least one other person who is sufficiently knowledgeable to assess its value must give it a sniff test. If you are an IT project manager and somebody on the team reports to you that they finished their spec, and they email it to you, you yourself may not be able to assess the quality of it due to a lack of technical expertise. For example, if you are not an automobile mechanic and somebody lifts the hood of your car and tells you the carburetor has been replaced and installed properly, that person could be wrong about that, and you wouldn't know. You either have to trust the mechanic blindly or else trust the car repair service center by reputation. Please do not trust any IT consulting firm by reputation (unless you have a long-standing relationship, and they are a known quantity to you).

You must have an objective third party who can look over design documents and spot a problem before it's too late. You must discover early on in the project any IT resources that are failure points and replace them. The only way to discover this, other than something overt such as the person showing up drunk and getting into fist fights with the client, is to peer review their design documents. A clue that an IT resource is incompetent is that they don't write any documents at all. A second clue is that their documents are of poor quality. These are your two main clues. Remember them and use them well. What other way would you know that the people you are paying big bucks to work on your IT project are not ever going to get it done? You see them in cubicles or talking on Zoom calls and think everything is fine.

The ONLY yardstick of competence you have early on in the project is the progress on design artifacts. Why is this rarely ever checked? Please, don't make that crucial mistake.

Upon discovering that your IT system designers are incapable of writing a decent design document, what should you do? You may not like this answer, but we are obliged to give it. The answer is that you must replace them. That is all you can do. You don't have time to mentor them into being able to learn a profession. If the person is a junior, paid at a low rate, who is apprenticing with a senior designer, then mentoring is fine, but if there is no senior that is going to get the work done, while junior looks on, that won't work. Understand that the IT system must be designed, otherwise it will never go live. Understand also that without a competent designer that system (or that part of the system) will never get designed, and hence, will never go live. This stuff does not happen magically or by wishful thinking.

You cannot project manage an incompetent resource to learn a profession in the course of an IT project; that is impossible. You can project manage an already competent professional towards achieving better results. We have seen incompetent IT designers who fail to come up with any decent design artifacts continue to participate in IT projects for months and years at a time without any reaction from project managers or operational managers. We have seen IT experts who know what they are doing, raising red flags when encountering incompetent resources, only to be slapped on the wrist for not being "team players" by project managers, operational managers, and consulting firm partners who are trying to make peace at all costs and avoid unpleasantries. What we have seen less seldom is bad IT resources getting removed from projects at the early stages. Instead, they keep the rotten apples, despite the fact that the worms have been identified, and wait until the entire tree is dead. The bad IT resources are removed from the project, when there is no project left, because the entire thing has tanked. This is the norm.

When staffing a baseball team, you send out scouts to look for already great players. You don't have the time or the luxury to create good players. Good players were created in sandlots, high school, college, and minor leagues. You are spending millions of dollars. This is the major leagues. You need to cut players who cannot perform. This is the harsh reality. Why is this almost never done until it is too late? Before there is any acknowledgment of incompetence, the project is hopelessly behind schedule and way over budget or worse yet, already scrapped. You can't afford to make that mistake.

Reduce the number of documents. One big "bible" of a document that contains the entire design in one place is one-stop-shopping to get answers and verify what was decided upon. The "bible" is the blueprint for the project (or phase of a project). Allow the documents to be organized in any way the author wants. Delete obsolete documents from your servers. Delete or move older versions of documents to an archive or backup folder. Keep your folders clean. Have only a small handful of living documents. Make sure everybody on the project knows exactly where those documents live. Avoid complicated nested folder structures wherever you store the documents. Keep it simple.

As you are holding meetings, go right into those "living documents" and update them on the fly. Don't use the Microsoft Word change tracking feature. Don't save the history of every stupid sentence in the document; don't be that anal retentive. Don't overcomplicate things. Make decisions now, then just record the decision immediately in the document, right then and there. Delete paragraphs that no longer apply. Nobody needs a history of what you decided against. Make a full-court-press on finishing a design document that can be used as a build order to stand up a module or functional area.

You can store your documents inside of applications, be they project management applications or collaboration tools. You don't need to use a network folder or folder on a cloud storage site or Microsoft SharePoint. You can get creative as to how you store these documents and what form they take, but the important point is that you must "capture" the design somewhere and have it readily available with no confusion as to whether it is current.

A functional design document should be human readable. It should not be Excel grids with no explanation of anything. You need to write a prose blurb at the start of each section that explains what is going on, provides some context, and doesn't assume the reader has worked at that company for forty-years and therefore has all the tribal knowledge in their head. Tell the reader what the acronyms stand for. If you mention a software application, then you should provide a website URL link to that company's website so that there will be no doubt what you are referring to. Describe, describe, describe, and describe. Explain, explain, explain, and then explain it again. Name names. Go ahead and list people by names, such as Anil in the warehouse, or Guillermo in the controller's office. List their titles, phone numbers, and where they work. Add lots of screen shots. Put arrows, captions, and highlights on the screen shots to make them even easier to understand. Create diagrams using PowerPoint, Visio, or a similar tool, and add those in as visual aids. Hire people that know how to write good design documents and your project will very likely succeed.

Read the design documents yourself. If you can't make heads or tails out of them, then guess what? The people creating them are not skilled enough to write a good design document and that means they are also not skilled enough to stand up a new IT system. This is the blunt reality you need to face. Wake up! Your IT project failed, because you didn't review the design documents, or have some other third-party expert review them for you. Next time, insist on great design documents and read them carefully or have a trusted expert review them for you.

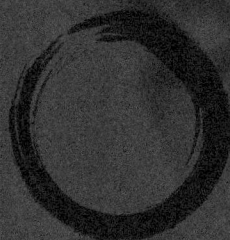

The Zen of IT Manifesto

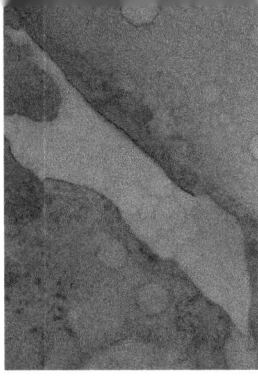

The 3 Core Concepts

Core Concept #1: Embrace Change

Before we make any large-scale digital transformation plans, we prepare our organization, our data, and our people. We prepare our organization by examining and simplifying our business rules and company policies. We prepare our data by cleansing it in the legacy system. We prepare our people by taking change management seriously. This is what we do before we even make any kind of IT project plan.

Core Concept #2: Seek Balance

When formulating any large-scale digital transformation plan, we generally avoid a big bang approach, and instead phase the transformation by module or functional area or some other creative approach; these are our go-live project phases. Within each go-live project phase we must cut scope drastically down to the bare bones essential features needed for go live, leaving bells and whistles and nice-to-haves to be added later during continuous process improvement. Within each project go-live phase we must go through each and every step of implementation methodology phases. This is how we arrive at an IT project plan that is realistic and feasible, instead of a "mission impossible" which is doomed to failure at the outset.

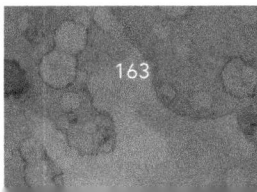

Core Concept #3: Act as One

When delivering on any large-scale digital transformation project, we staff the project with sufficient IT talent, valuing well-rounded known quantities over app experts. We free up super-user resources by back filling their position and/or hiring new internal resources that can focus 100% on the project. Our meetings are conducted by IT systems designers as a logical series of questions. Designers go off by themselves and design, then regroup with managers and users for iterative feedback sessions. Decisions are made and documented. Prototype apps are preferred where possible, but it is peer reviewed non-boilerplate design documentation that is the primary proof of project progress. Early on in the project, we replace any resources that cannot produce quality design documents. We simplify and streamline our documentation standards, avoiding rigid, formal, and onerous templates and limit our document types to a few key living documents stored in an easily accessible place known to all. This is how we effectively and efficiently execute our realistic and feasible IT project plan.

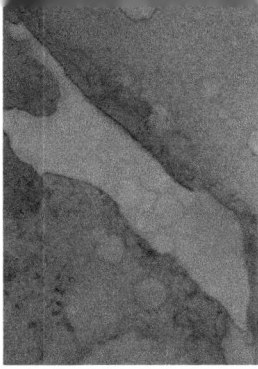

The 9 Core Concept Components

Core Concept Component #1: Simplify Our Lives

Simplification, not sophistication or complication, is the hallmark of effectiveness and prosperity. Examine and simplify your business rules and organizational policies well ahead of embarking on an IT digital transformation initiative.

Core Concept Component #2: Enrich Us All

Investment in digital transformation is no longer optional. You must keep up with advances in computer technology just to survive. Your return on investment is your continued existence. Information is not God and is not even good. Limit your reporting requirements to a reasonable and useful level of granularity.

Core Concept Component #3: Empower Our Future

End-users are rarely the reason for IT project failure. IT consultants may give bad advice. But usually, the fault lies with top management. Top management must get involved, set aside an adequate budget including a budget for change management, set a realistic timeframe, and be unified in their insistence that the new system is not optional, but necessary for survival. End-users must not be granted veto authority nor allowed by management to engage in bad behavior or to adopt bad attitudes.

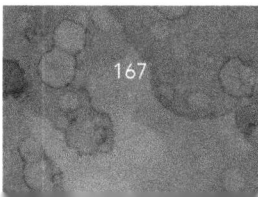

Core Concept Component #4: Prune Our Garden

You cannot buy a new IT system. You can only guide the evolution of your existing legacy system. Reduce feature scope to the minimum required functionality and consider advanced features to be continuous process improvement goals to be added after go-live.

Core Concept Component #5: Phase Our Journey

Be humble and patient. Big-bang projects are seductive, but seldom work. Phasing by functional area or module may be necessary. Throw-away integration coding may be necessary. Going live with less features than the legacy system may be necessary. The hallmark of success are go-lives. A project phase is a go-live. A go-live may be just one department or module going live. For every go-live you must go through all the implementation methodology phases. With a big bang you only need to go through the implementation methodology phases once and that would be great if big bangs worked, but most often they do not, and in fact, the big-bang approach is the number one reason for large-scale IT system implementation failure.

Core Concept Component #6: Manage Our Miracle

Lean and Agile project management methodologies are a vast improvement over the traditional waterfall approach, but even a well-executed Lean or Agile project plan is not enough. Agile was developed for software development companies to be more efficient at coding commercial software for the software market. However, most wasteful IT spending occurs when clerical end-users fail to adopt already coded software platforms. Development and implementation are two very different matters. Large-scale software platform implementations rarely fail because of poorly executed project management, but rather, they fail due to a lack of lack of change management, failing to examine and then simplify business rules and company policies upfront, neglecting to cleanse your data well in advance of the project, and mostly due to a lack of humility and patience which leads to unrealistic, underfunded, mission impossible big bang project plans.

Core Concept Component #7: Free Our People

Hire enough top-notch IT talent and vet all of them. Free up super-user subject matter experts 100% from day-to-day operations, by back filling their position or through a new hire. High-level managers such as VP's and C-Levels should be enforcing change, cheerleading, and have skin in the game. Make sure you have client-side project management to act as a watchdog instead of relying on an external consulting firm to manage the project by themselves.

Core Concept Component #8: Meet to Act

A methodical top-down systematic approach, where a list of topics is gathered through a focused line of questioning with the goal of constructing a high-level hierarchical outline, with details being artfully added at a reasonable and appropriate level of granularity must be followed regardless of what kind of IT system you are designing, and regardless of which implementation methodology phase you are in, and regardless of which go-live project phase you are working on, and regardless of which type of document is being authored. Every kind of design meeting, no matter where you are in the process, requires a focused, logical, orderly inquiry and decision-making process with the goal of making decisions, writing down the findings or building a prototype or mock-up as the concrete results of the meeting.

Core Concept Component #9: Write to Read

When it comes to large-scale IT platform implementation and adoption, the primary measure of progress is not working software, as Agile principles might have you believe and as may be the case when coding commercial software at a software development company, but rather, it is peer-reviewed non-boilerplate functional and technical design artifacts. Simplify and streamline your documentation process. Reduce the number of design document types to a few key document types. Allow designers to use their own document outlines rather than adhering to onerous rigid templates. Store a limited number of one-stop-shopping design "blueprints" in a very visible and easily accessible place that everyone on the project knows about. Update the design document in design feedback meetings and delete obsolete sections and prior versions. Have a few key "living documents" that are up-to-date and comprehensive. If your IT system designers are not creating quality design artifacts, replace them immediately.

Ask
Andy

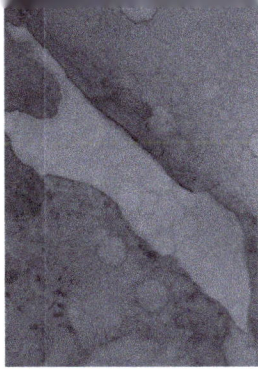

Ask Andy

In this Q&A section, Andy imparts his wisdom borne of decades of success-ful partnering with a multitude of clients in a wide array of industries by envisioning and executing on business software implementations and digital transformations.

Q&A

We're a relatively small organization. We barely have enough of a budget to replace our outdated IT systems. Do we really need to hire a change management consultant, or run some kind of internal change management campaign? If the new system is so much better than the old one, and it better be, won't users want to adopt it?

> *People do not accept what they do not understand. Personal discomfort yields organizational disharmony. Design the adoption before embarking on the design.*

Our IT systems are unsupported and badly in need of upgrade or replacement. We don't have time to examine and simply our business policies, accounting rules, and the like. We need a new system now. Why can't we just incorporate policy changes into the implementation of our new platforms?

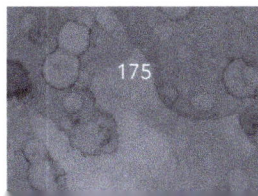

Delve deep, gaze wide, see from higher places. Your organization is a tangled knot. A rope that is taut will provide passage across the chasm.

Our company policies, business rules, and accounting methods have evolved to what they are today over several decades and they really can't be changed. Complexity is inherent in our particular industry. Isn't this new software so advanced and automated that it has the features and capabilities to simplify our business process workstreams despite the complexity inherent in our organization and our industry?

In nature, the series of actions taken to achieve a particular outcome flow along well-worn channels carved by time. In business, the vagaries of history are written into the backward compatibility which chokes the life out of profitability. Major surgery is required to restore health where major arteries are blocked.

Our investors demand growth quarter after quarter. We need to venture into new markets and expand our offerings. Isn't it foolhardy to worry about the administrative cost and IT cost of doing business in a new area or new way when that new venture could explode into our biggest source of revenue, and our IT systems will eventually scale to reduce the cost per transaction to a negligible amount?

If we drill deep enough into any dirt, we find the precious treasures which mother nature hides. Our time and our labor is rewarded. But we must reckon the cost of this labor for the accumulation of profit is not merely the increase of sales. IT costs are hidden in more obscure places than a pirate's plunder.

We've run our business on a proprietary homegrown application for the last 30 years. The data is not even in a modern database. It's really hard to get at. We just need to start afresh with a new system. There is no point trying to clean up the old data in the old system. It's too far gone. Is it really necessary to make an effort to clean up the legacy data; after all, the new system is going to replace all that?

> *Feed the cats that dwell in the house you live in today for every manner of vermin are stow aways to your next destination.*

There are tax laws, bank loan covenants, and legal implications to consider. Our organization is divided into many different separate legal entities for good reasons. We'll have to involve our legal department, our auditors, and the members of the board. Trying to sort out our legal entity structure and hierarchy is going to derail our IT project, and that structure is set in stone anyway. Isn't the new software capable of automated consolidations? Why is this such a big deal?

> *Each legal entity that you add is a child born into a family of sibling rivalries. It is another mouth to feed. One pot of soup feeds many children. But each child must work the fields to fill the pot with greens.*

The way we price our products and services is something we give a great deal of attention to. We have examined those policies very deeply and continuously. It's just the nature of the beast, our pricing and our customer rebate structure is super complex. Isn't the reason we're putting in a new more powerful billing system so that we can easily handle our complex pricing model, and other sophisticated business rules?

You examined a complex business process and then tailored software to match that process. You have automated the complex process. It is no longer manual. It is no longer paper. Doing so was expensive and the cost of maintaining it is ongoing and considerable. What would have happened if, instead, you had eliminated that complex process? Would your customers be lost? Would your vendors cease to serve you? Would you be out of business? Or would you be more profitable, perhaps with lower revenue but higher margins?

What you think you need is only what you have become accustomed to, not what you actually need to turn a healthy profit.

Our back-office accounting software system may be old, but it is very stable, and it is highly tailored to our needs. Yes, it's an outdated operating system and technology but it works. Why go through the trouble, risk, pain, and cost to try to replace that?

The thought of replacing or upgrading your back-office accounting software is daunting for many companies. It might seem easier to stick with what you're currently doing. However, there are several reasons why this is a death sentence for your business. Here are the key reasons to replace your ERP system:

- Obsolete technology – Your back-office accounting software is working but it was built on top of very old technology. You may be stuck dealing with inefficient technology and infrastructure, and it's adversely affecting your bottom line. IT personnel are relegated to 24/7 maintenance of the legacy system and are always fighting fires, never allowing your company to strategically plan for the future.

- Lack of features - Legacy systems require numerous bolt-on solutions in order to function, and these many systems don't always speak well to each other. You need a new modern back-office accounting system fully integrated to your front-office system, billing system and more. A single version of the truth for every employee ensures that everyone is making decisions based on accurate, real-time data.

- End of support – Many ERP providers will soon begin to discontinue support for previous versions, leaving you with several expensive options. You could take their offer to upgrade to the latest platform, but as soon as you finally upgrade your outdated system, it will be time for more maintenance costs, reduced vendor support and yet another upgrade. It's a vicious cycle.

- Maintenance cost - It's inevitable. By the time you spend countless time and dollars upgrading your legacy back-office accounting system, there will no doubt be another upgrade just around the corner. Your company is stuck in "revision prison" and suffers from downtime and unhappy customers, neither of which bodes well for the long-term success of your business.

Our IT spending, as a percentage of net revenue, is within industry norms, and to keep it within those boundaries, we cannot embark on a replacement of our front-office or back-office system at this time. Maintaining and supporting what we have consumes our entire IT budget. Our products are getting out the door, our orders are getting processed, our vendors are getting paid. Is digital transformation really so important?

In the stone age men fought with rocks. In the bronze age, bronze. In the iron age, iron. In the computer age war is waged in silicon.

ROI calculations are never a perfect model of reality. We get that. But we can't just spend blindly. We need to justify every investment we make. When we looked at moving our CRM and ERP to the cloud, the numbers just didn't add up. Aren't there more important things to spend money on, like employee training programs, additional sales reps, and new equipment?

Move to the cloud. Do this now. The cloud is where everything will be. If you do not go there soon, then there will be no company left with which to calculate anything.

We continue to invest in new IT systems with a focus on customer facing technology such as our ecommerce platform, and our primary goal is to get users more access to more information. How can anyone say that more information isn't a good thing?

The quantity of information is irrelevant and misleading. Quality is all that matters. Quality information makes for a good customer experience. Speed. Convenience. Consistency. Friendliness. And Human Touch. All hallmarks of quality.

The business world is getting more and more complicated, and timeframes are getting squeezed. Customers are demanding mobile apps with more information that gets instantly updated. These days how can anyone be advocating for IT systems that serve up less information?

Serve up more quality information. Eliminate the static. A global digital transformation is underway, forcing companies to change their business models and adapt to a new reality. It is not the companies that are driving this change. This change is being driven by the customer. Today, customers expect relevant content in relation to what they are doing anytime, anywhere and in the format and on the device of their choosing. It is their journey that should dictate your strategy. To keep pace your business must embrace technology that can deliver an always-connected customer experience.

Our digital transformation project has failed, and we are in the process of starting it up again. We have already lost a lot of time and don't have the luxury of a pre-planning phase in which we examine our business policies and cleanse data in our legacy system. What can we do?

A house of straw and sticks will be blown over by any wind. Take whatever time necessary to gather good clay and form strong bricks.

We operate in a very specific industry niche. There are only a few software providers who cater to this niche. Everybody uses them. We hired them to upgrade our system. They know what to do. We feel we are in good hands. The users understand that the system is getting upgraded. This is an IT issue. What do the CEO and CFO have to do with this?

In war, generals concern themselves with all matters that could affect the outcome of battle. Your organization is in a battle for survival in the computer age. Your organization must extend itself digitally or face certain extinction. Your top brass is riding into battle mounted atop your IT systems.

It's getting harder and harder to retain good employees. The last thing we can do is force them to use a system that doesn't meet their needs. The users need to be empowered to set the requirements. How can we force users to adopt a system that was designed without their authority?

> *A bus driver who knows the route and obeys the traffic laws is needed to transport people safely around the city. This bus driver has no authority to change the route, nor the skill and experience to design a highway system.*

Top management at our company has no choice but to focus on day-to-day operations. We operate in a very competitive marketplace and conditions change on a daily basis. There is always a fire to put out. We have a solid internal IT department who engages IT consultants to upgrade our systems and we trust them to get it done. We're paying enough. How can you expect top management to find the time to run IT projects?

> *We are not suggesting that top management run your IT projects on a day-to-day basis. However, the business and IT executives need to share their top strategies for creating realistic schedules and keeping projects on track. A few key areas which top management needs to be aware of and plan and execute well on include:*

- Working with your service partner and vendors to put together the right team
- Devising a realistic timeline
- Setting and acknowledging milestones
- Receiving regular updates from the project manager
- Having protocols in place to manage issues
- Being honest and taking action when things go wrong

Our users are creatures of habit. They have been using the same system for decades. Realistically speaking, we are going to need to customize the new system extensively before it will meet their needs. We understand the cost and have factored that in. What's so bad about that?

Tinkering with the inside clockworks of your wristwatch may quiet the ticking sound but you are likely to find yourself late to your next meeting, and in need of a new watch.

It shouldn't take so long and cost so much money to replace our IT systems with cloud apps. Consulting firms overcharge. The fault is the consultants and the software developers. They always charge too much. It's a racket. Given this reality, is there really any way to win?

Victory equates to acceptance which leads us to realistic goals and time-frames. The client who is patient, practical and honest cannot be fooled into signing up for a fleecing. Flowing with the natural course of the river we arrive at our destination keenly aware and refreshed.

We worked on a big IT transformation project for more than a year. In the end it was a bust. Our users attended all the meetings, and our top management was behind the project. The consultants never really understood our business. Is there any way to ensure you're selecting the right implementers?

When choosing a new system or solution and service provider for your business, one size does not fit all. While the software must address and satisfy industry-specific needs for functionality, scalability, and complexity, the service provider should have a proven track record helping companies like yours achieve the operational excellence required to realize optimal profitability and grow the business. The right implementation partner is needed to bring the software to life. Here is a brief outline of what to look for when selecting an implementation partner:

- First, select the software that best addresses your industry and company's specific needs. A good start is to ensure that the provider can support all the capabilities that are unique to your industry and that the software serves as a robust development platform so that you can augment the capabilities with any unique needs you may have. It's always good to look at the number and caliber of both solution partners and 3rd party ISVs (independent software vendors).

- Define the selection criteria with system stakeholders: Is geographical proximity important? Do I need custom development capabilities? What kind of support turnaround times do I need? Does the service provider have any other capabilities I might need (staff augmentation, etc.)? What's the financial viability of the service provider? Then determine if each of these criteria are "must haves" or "nice to haves".

- Shortlist the top services partners that have deep experience with your selected technology, then go through a discovery process to see how each of them measures up against your criteria. Start with the evaluation of no more than three providers. More can become unwieldy.

- Be certain that the provider has the ability to support other systems you may have in place, as you likely have a CRM (customer relationship management) as well as business intelligence tools that will require some data integration. It is also useful to ensure that the provider has a great track record with other ISV solutions that you may need, either now or in the future.

- Check references and evaluate them with a discerning eye. Think about both the similarities and the differences between your situation and that of the reference.
- Most of all, be certain that you and your team can develop open and effective communication channels with the implementation partner. This relationship is likely to be a long one, and a major foundation for a successful project is effective communication.

We know that our IT project failed because our users kept insisting that the new system must work like the old system. Also, they failed to reveal all the requirements during the discovery and analysis. We are determined not to let that happen again. How can we make sure that this time things will be different?

To succeed in your IT project, you must embed business analysts who are free from day-to-day operational duties in all your departmental areas, not just the usual harried clerical workers, and that probably means new hires. A few good new hires will make a big difference.

With the money we're paying for this new system we expect the functionality and capabilities to far exceed what we have today. How could we possibly explain to our users, our shareholders, and our top management, that we intend to introduce a new system with less features?

More does not mean better. Bells and whistles make an enticing trap. Stay on task, stay true to your core needs, and get the key parts of your new system live and stable before adding more functional areas and features. To support the long-term implementation of your new system, start by prioritizing those capabilities that need to be mastered first.

If we aren't going to get a ton more features and a ton more automation, then we might as well stay on the old system. When we revamp our IT systems, we intend to demand a higher level of functionality. That just makes sense. Isn't expecting less features defeatism and pessimism?

The most urgent reason for changing systems is that the current system is inhibiting the business in some way. This requires strategic planning but here are a few things you should consider before you decide to stay on the old system.

- Does the old system lack functionality or flexibility which may be limiting your growth or agility?
- Does the old system suffer from slow response time and difficulty in accessing information?
- How is your existing hardware infrastructure? Does it become unreliable, and support limited and increasingly expensive as the equipment is discontinued or the supplier is acquired or goes out of business?
- What is the true cost of the maintenance of your legacy system? Does it become increasingly expensive to maintain for the same reasons listed above?
- Is your legacy system falling behind with regard to market technology advances and industry sector standards?

User frustration and complaints, and the business difficulties that are a direct result of system shortcomings, will likely lead to a system replacement project. Sometimes, however, a company is just unhappy with their current system. Often, this is because the system was never completely and successfully implemented and therefore has never gained the confidence of users or become a valued resource. In some of these cases, continuous process improvement is a wiser and less expensive approach than moving to another software platform.

The minimal required functionality just puts us right back to where we are now. If we take that approach then after a year of hard work, disruptions to our operations, and so much upheaval, we will have nothing to show for it. The requirements cannot be minimal. How can we ensure project success and still ensure that we deliver capabilities that meet all our requirements?

A snake does not have legs but travels frequently and eats well.

Our users are uploading and downloading data all over the place. There are so many integrations and data interfaces. They use so many different technologies. There are Excel files, flat files, web portals, several types of middleware, EDI, and manual uploads. If we change anything, the whole thing falls apart and it's so unpredictable. How can we move forward?

One of the primary purposes for a new system such as ERP is to automate business processes to make the business more efficient and provide better visibility into those processes. But to get the benefits of ERP systems, businesses need to integrate their ERP system with their other enterprise systems. This can often be difficult, and the challenges of ERP integration involve both the age of the systems, the architecture of these systems, and the need to integrate new applications and systems into the original ERP. The common phrase, "United we stand, divided we fall," applies here. It's also a great example of why ERP integration is key to running a successful business. Integration is a way of connecting ERP software to other systems to ensure that consistent information is shared while also automating workflows. There are a few different methods of implementing the integrations. The best system integration option for you is dependent on your specific business and can be affected by factors such as the current systems you are using, your integration budget and whether you use on-premises software, a cloud-based solution, or some hybrid of both. Here are some of the integration approaches that you may consider:

- Point-to-point: In a point-to-point integration, the ERP software is individually connected to each software or tool. The difficulty with this method is that you must conduct an integration separately for each system that you wish to use. Additionally, the process can become complicated quickly as more and more tools are added. However, some companies opt to go with point-to-point because it has a reasonably low barrier to entry.

- Custom applications: Some companies might choose to build their own customized applications or adapters to integrate their various business tools. Custom applications often start with data transfer capabilities but may grow to encompass more tasks and workflows. Custom applications have a similar issue as point-to-point integration in that it can be challenging to maintain as a company grows and adds more tools to its software portfolio.

- Enterprise Middleware: Applications are connected by a "communication bus", such as Microsoft Azure Logic Apps, BizTalk, MuleSoft, Dell Boomi, etc. The bus serves as a centralized tool where the applications communicate. The benefit of doing integration this way is that other apps don't have to be tweaked when another component is added – the bus centralizes all the communications. This is a more straightforward process than using custom applications or point-to-point integration. Today most enterprise middleware offers a large set of out-of-the-box connectors which help orchestrate the communication between different systems and make data integrations much easier to develop.

It's essential that you keep these potential integration challenges in mind when selecting and adapting the solution that's right for you.

We really must succeed in this go round. We are willing to cut our feature scope down to the minimal required functionality in all our functional areas. The problem is how do you determine what is truly required versus what's a nice-to-have?

First, conduct research and document your current business processes, pain points, and strengths. Think ahead and consider what your business workflow processes will look like in the future. What is the reason a new IT system is needed? What are the problems a new IT system will solve? This work will help you outline requirements later. Secondly, identify the key stakeholders who need to contribute to the IT system evaluation requirements. Skipping this step may cause you to miss a key requirement or functionality. Including many voices in the technology evaluation process will deliver high user adoption of the solution after implementation. Key considerations for IT system requirements include:

- What are your business goals for the next few years?
- Which areas of the business are growing, and which are shrinking?
- How could a new IT system benefit your company?
- Do you have sufficient budget set aside for digital transformation?
- What does a successful implementation look like for our organization?

We are making major investments in our IT capabilities. We have a large budget set aside. We expect and demand more functionality at go-live and we are willing to pay for it. If we throw enough resources at this project, we can get it done in a short timeframe. Am I missing something here?

Well, you mentioned two important pieces which is good – the money and the resources, but that may not be sufficient to ensure the success of your IT project. For example, you will also need (a) support from executives, it's vital that your executive team is on board with your IT project, especially for a large scale and / or transformation project (b) Clearly define your project scope – even if you have a large budget and a proper team for the project, having a well-defined and written scope of work can mean the difference between a failed project with disastrous results, and a highly successful project with huge benefits. Your project scope is the basis for the requirements of the project and the resources that need to be deployed. Don't skimp on scoping. It pays to spend the time upfront making sure everything is documented and to clearly define expectations upfront and establish overall goals (c) Proactive change management - it's important to build in enough time to train people on new systems and processes.

Don't let end users feel like they just swapped an old, clunky headache for a newer, shinier headache and (d) an implementation partner who knows your industry - to help monitor and guide your project's success, you should consider working with a system implementation partner who knows your industry as well as they know the software.

How can we limit features when our users insist that they won't be able to keep up with the volume of transactions unless we provide as much or more automation at go-live than they have now?

When you're planning the implementation of your new IT system, you may find yourself falling into one of the worst traps of IT system implementation, the one-more-feature spiral. You want it to be perfect, so you're thinking of all the cool features that would help to achieve this perfection, and so the list keeps growing. You know what they say: more is more, right? Well, no, it's not. There are features that are certain must-haves but there are some that will turn out to be useless. Instead of implementing every possible suggestion, you should focus on the right time to quality ratio. Prioritizing the features for your minimum viable product is the key. Defining and documenting your business requirements aids in the selection process by evaluating requirements in terms of "Must-Have" versus "Nice-to-Have"- focusing on features that offer a competitive advantage, are industry-specific, or optimize currently problematic business processes, such as automations. This will help your project management team prioritize your requirements for the new system selection by keeping a perspective on what is truly essential.

Our system is all inter-connected. It's impossible to phase in by module or department. Clearly, we will need to replace the whole system all at once. It may be difficult, but we have no choice. If we get everything ready ahead of time and provide proper training what's so wrong about a big bang approach?

Clients have many choices to make during each phase of your system implementation. One of the most important choices takes place right at the beginning. Before you dive too far into the process, you'll need to decide if you want to use a phased approach or go live with everything all at once. The latter is referred to as a big bang implementation. While it can work well for some organizations, it isn't always recommended for others. The term "big bang implementation" is used to describe a go-live scenario where a business switches from its existing system to a new solution at a single point in time. This means all the company's modules and offices go live simultaneously. Big bang implementations work best for organizations that only have one or two functional areas that will be using the new software. In addition, robust system testing and data validation techniques are a must-have with a big bang implementation, as they can help identify and resolve bugs or compatibility issues before go-live. Despite the risks, the big bang approach does have plenty of benefits. Chiefly, companies that successfully manage a big bang implementation enjoy a quicker and lower-cost process than companies that spread the implementation out over a longer period. Finally, if the overall project cost is an overriding concern, a big-bang strategy may be appealing because it eliminates the cost of operating old and new systems at the same time. However, keep in mind that the big bang approach is only advisable where it is truly feasible. If you are not honest, realistic, and knowledgeable enough to accurately gauge the feasibility, then you are at risk of a scrapped project. The cost of a scrapped project, a re-reorganization, and then starting again from scratch is much more expensive than a long-term phased approach.

We can't integrate with our legacy system. It's so old that there is no easy way to get data in or out of it. How are we supposed to replace only certain modules or business functions in the legacy system if we can't get the new software to talk to the old software?

Companies that implement a new system should start by analyzing their legacy systems. Just because a company adopts new technology, it doesn't make the previous software useless. Once a business thoroughly analyzes its existing system, discovers flaws in processes, creates realistic goals for new solutions and concludes simple fixes are out of the question, the company should obtain new software from a software vendor or authorized partner. If possible, though, the business should not get rid of its legacy system. To prepare a legacy system for the new system implementation, IT professionals must first clean the existing data. Employees must check for any redundant or incorrect information. Both systems must operate with uniform definitions and business terms. If managers want the tools to work together, systems have to speak the same language. As integration proceeds, the implementation team should look out for overlap. Old and new solutions probably provide a few similar functions. If the legacy system offers a feature that still works efficiently, there may be no need to change it.

We hired a consulting company to implement our IT system for us. They say that they replace entire systems all the time. We have several good references for them. They also tell us that the quickest and therefore least expensive way to get us to the cloud is to replace all modules and functional areas all at once on the same go-live day. They developed the software they are implementing. How could they be mistaken?

You cannot climb an acorn.

If we break our project into go-lives of only certain departments, modules, or functions, the project will take too long. We will need to go through every single implementation methodology phase of design, build, training, cutover planning, etc. over and over again for each small go-live. That seems more disruptive than a big bang approach and what a waste of time! If we have to keep doing all these mini go-lives, isn't that just a whole lot of extra work for no good reason?

The two most common methodologies for implementing an IT project are "big bang" and phased rollout. Big bang is a "one-and-done" deal - the system goes live across all departments on a predetermined date. Despite its name, a substantial amount of planning goes on in advance. Prior to deployment, management must determine any organizational changes necessary to make the system viable, employees must receive adequate training on the new system, data stewards must convert and import information from the old system to the new system, and the technical staff must conduct trial runs to verify the validity of the software. In contrast, a phased rollout implements the new system in a series of steps. An organization may deploy individual modules one at a time, starting with its core processes, or it may introduce the new system to a particular business unit or site before deploying the software to its other departments or locations. The following are advantages of a phased rollout:

- Low Risk. Because there's no hard-and-fast deadline, the organization can adjust as needed during the transition
- Steady Performance. The organization has more time to train employees, and employees have more time to adjust to the new system.

Certainly, there are some disadvantages with the phased rollout approach too – for example, it lacks focus, deployment occurs over an extended period, and staff must concentrate on a single module or department at a time rather than on the system as a whole. Secondly, the cost is high. The organization must devote resources to maintaining the old system and the new system as well as any temporary interfaces used to link the two systems. Unfortunately, there is no simple answer to tell you which methodology is better or not, the best way to determine which strategy is best for your organization is to assess factors such as initial costs, operating expenses, ROI, and impact on productivity. Then, consider how each approach may affect business operations. One approach might appear better than the other on paper, but those advantages might not apply in the real world. In the real world, unexpected delays and complications arise continuously; this is why a phased approach is more of a sure bet, but it requires more patience. True, a successful big bang is better than a successful phased approach, but a successful phased approach is better than a failed big bang.

We have phased our project by location. That's what obviously makes the most sense. Yes, each location is in a sense a big bang, but it's manageable because it is limited to only one location. If we then try to phase at each location, the project will take way too long, right?

Under a phased approach, the deployment of features, tools and components is done over an extended period, which may cover weeks or months. This more measured approach can be less risky than the big-bang strategy. It also enables the company to focus first on "quick wins"—the functions that deliver the most immediate benefits—and to apply learnings from the initial deployment phases to improve the process for subsequent phases.

Your approach is to phase the rollout by geography / location or facilities. You can certainly implement the phased approach at each location and may start with core functions and expand from there. Once the solution is being implemented, tested, and considered as "perfect" at one location, you can decide to mimic the same solution and move on to other offices, manufacturers, or facilities. Certainly, the duration of the project will be extended but in the final analysis your risk is greatly reduced.

You talk about establishing a robust data integration middleware platform and a business intelligence reporting platform up-front as a preliminary phase of a financial or operational software implementation. That's really going to slow down the project. Doesn't it make more sense to adopt those new platforms as a later phase, sometime after go-live?

Integration middleware is your translator. Business intelligence is your scout. At the outset of your journey take with you a well-versed translator and an eagle-eyed scout.

We have already committed to, communicated, and agreed on standing up our new IT system all at once. We don't like to call it a big bang. We call it a holistic approach. We left out the nice-to-haves and are considering all those non-critical features as continuous process improvement goals for the future. It's impossible to change our plans now and try to break up the project by module, department, function or whatever. That would involve way too much extra planning and needless complexity. We already cut scope drastically, so isn't that enough?

"I want it all and I want it now!", one of my clients told me. And hey, what's wrong with that? Sometimes nothing at all but let's talk about implementing a new IT system. The big bang or what you called holistic approach is wanting it all right now. Turn everything on all at once, one go-live date for the entire scope of the project. There are reasons why this might make sense. Sometimes it's driven by transactions such as divestitures and acquisitions where the entire population in scope has to be converted to the new system or added to existing systems by a certain date or you may risk incurring penalties. Or your current systems may no longer be supported at some point, and you are forced to move large parts or all of our environment to new systems. And sometimes it is simply the business case that drives the justification for getting new systems. If everything isn't transitioned all at once, we can't afford the project. And sometimes let's face it, we might "choose" this approach based on pressure from the C-suite to go big bang because after all, it "shouldn't be that hard".

While these are all reasons to take the Big Bang / Holistic approach, in our experience this is usually less desirable than taking a more measured and controlled, Phased approach. In the Phased approach, analysis is done up front to determine logical bite sized chunks of the project that can be sequenced in the move from the current landscape to the new one. The obvious advantage of staging the project in manageable chunks is the mitigation of risk. By tackling smaller chunks of work, problems that you may encounter can be smaller, more quickly isolated with fewer variables and corrected quickly at the point of go-live. Furthermore, moving one controllable chunk of work at a time will also reduce the change management challenge. The obvious drawback to phased over big bang might be that a phased approach will take longer to complete. However, that may not always be the case. When working in a big bang approach the coordination of testing across the project can be complicated and take longer than expected. Sometimes phasing out the work results in efficiencies and the end date isn't all that different from the big bang approach.

While both approaches have their justifications and pros and cons, the phased approach tends to be far less risky. If you're debating these approaches in your own project, get an external strategy consultant to come in and work with you on objectively laying out the risks and timing of each approach to set your project up for success before you even start. In other words, don't assume a big bang approach at the outset of the project and during the contract negotiations. Don't sign on the dotted line to commit to a big bang. Instead, sign up for a smaller less committed, less expensive mini project to study the requirements, define a scope, select a strategy (big bang versus phased, and then how to phase), and then make a plan, and finally, sign the full contract only after you have made an intelligent informed choice about whether to go big bang or phased. Don't simply assume big bang as the only option because it's supposedly "cheaper".

We are embarking on a challenging digital transformation project, but we are well positioned for success because we follow an Agile project management approach on all our projects. As long as we stick to the Agile principles what could go wrong?

Transformation projects are never easy. An Agile approach can help improve the results. For example, ERP solutions are a fundamental asset for most companies, and ERP transformations remain very time-consuming and complex. The Agile approach has the potential to dramatically streamline IT projects and in my experience in helping many organizations adopt Agile practices in a wide variety of situations, Agile when successfully applied to ERP methodologies, has resulted in quantifiably better results. Much of Agile's popularity is based on its results. Many research studies show that Agile organizations have a seventy percent chance of being in the top quartile of organizational health, the best indicator of long-term performance. Moreover, such companies simultaneously achieve greater customer centricity, faster time to market, higher revenue growth, lower costs, and a more engaged workforce. Specific to digital transformation, deploying a new IT system in an Agile way—irrespective of the underlying technology—translates into a range of tangible and intangible benefits:

- Reduction of program cost driven primarily by having to do less rework in the SIT (system integration testing) and UAT (user acceptance testing) phases
- Increase in the program's value by giving the product owner enough visibility into the project's progress to focus on high-value items
- Ability to compress workload into a given period through greater parallelization of functional teams
- Wider adoption of the solution by end users, as they are involved throughout the implementation
- Improvement in team morale, as they see the solution implementation's measurable progress every day

Transformation projects are always challenging, but these challenges can be far less daunting with an Agile approach.

Follow Agile principles by all means, but unless the scope can feasibly fit into the timeframe, no amount of agility will overcome the flawed strategy.

Our software implementation project has been a nightmare, and there are a lot of reasons for that, but in order to understand what went wrong and avoid repeating those same mistakes don't we need to just bring in more project managers and have them sort it out?

According to marketing studies, only 2.5% of companies complete 100% of their projects. The numbers are shocking, but they show the scale of the problem. Other studies show that 17% of IT projects go so badly, they threaten the existence of the business itself. So, who is to blame – managers, employers, or stakeholders? Or maybe it's the technology itself? There is no clear answer to this difficult question because the explanation is more complex. There are many reasons that contribute to the failure of IT projects in large organizations. To understand the complexity of the problem, it's crucial to understand the small parts that constitute it. Why? Because, in most cases, it's these minor elements that are an inseparable part of the main problem. Yet all the flaws that cause the failure of implementing technological projects can be easily avoided.

In order to do so, you need to identify them prior to starting the implementation process. And, to help you succeed, below is a list of 9 factors that contribute to the failure of IT projects in large organizations.

- Lack of involvement from senior management
- Gathering inaccurate requirements
- Poor communication between teams and project sponsors
- Lack of clearly defined objectives and milestones to measure progress
- Inaccurate estimates
- Limited resources

- Poor project management
- Undefined opportunities and unexpected risks
- Lack of review process

Project managers are your star players. Their job is to keep the project on track. They are the central figures in handling the day-to-day management tasks. To ensure project success, project managers must have the necessary skills, background, and qualifications. Your project manager can make or break the implementation process. However, you can see that it may not be helpful to just bring in more project managers and expect them to sort the issues out by themselves. There are many critical success factors which contribute to the success of the projects. Understanding the nine Core Concept Components of the Zen of IT and taking action based on what you have learned from this book will help you more than hiring more project managers.

Agile has evolved way beyond its roots as a software developer tool. The way we are adopting Agile project management principles is very sophisticated and far reaching. We feel confident that our project scope and our project phases are correct because they were arrived at through an Agile project management process. Our project plan calls for a roll out by subsidiary. Do we really need to take an extra step to phase each subsidiary by a smaller breakdown of mini go-lives? After all, we break up all our work into two-week long Agile sprints.

If each subsidiary or location has all the functional areas, such as Finance, Banking, Accounts Payable, Billing, and so on, then each subsidiary or location is a mini company with a complete system. Lots of big bangs are even worse than one big bang. If you centralize functions at headquarters and the subsidiary locations have relatively simple requirements, then phasing by location may be enough.

We'd like to hire more IT talent to work on our project, but the simple fact is that these people are hard to find. How can we staff the project with more IT talent when our recruiters can't find us any good candidates to interview?

The IT talent shortage presents one of the biggest obstacles to digital transformation. While it remains difficult to find employees with the requisite technical skills, the lack of soft skills prowess in areas like change management and collaboration is proving to be more of a challenge to modern-day digital transformation success. The shift in IT systems implementations from on premises to the cloud is also changing the mix of required skills that organizations need to maintain in-house. Rather than building up a staff of network and server experts or specialty programmers versed in specific application platforms, companies need to augment their teams to include IT experts fluent in business-oriented competencies, like operations optimization, change management, integration, and business process change, all skills that fall outside the scope of traditional business application internal technical support hires. You will need to make some tough choices and be patient. You may need to scale back your goals until you can hire or engage as consultants the necessary talent. It's better that you wait until you have the talent that you need than to start a costly project understaffed. This is a seldom considered advantage of taking a phased approach. A slower pace of go-lives means a less demanding recruiting requirement.

We've hired a top-tier consultancy to implement our new IT system. We have to trust them to staff the project according to their expertise and their knowledge of how to match requirements to skillsets among their staff. How can you expect us to vet their people, isn't that part of what we are paying them to do?

Most customers trust the consulting firm and don't bother to look at bios or try to vet their consultants in any way. This is foolish. You should demand that the consulting firm provides the names and bios of at least the most key consultants assigned to your project such as the overall solution architect. There are many ways you can vet consultants before you onboard them to your project:

- Learn about the consultant's background and qualifications. Look at the consultant's resume and bio, educational background, and certifications relevant to your project. It's a good sign if they seem willing to explore new learning opportunities and keep their skills updated.
- Ask the consultant about their hands-on experience. Hands-on experience is significant in the business world. Consider looking for consultants who have successfully completed similar projects in the past.
- Ensure their experience applies to your business. Look for consultants who have worked in your industry and with businesses that match yours in style, size, needs and goals.
- Examine their consulting track record. You don't just want a consultant with the right experience; you want a consultant who has demonstrated success with companies like yours. Ask for a portfolio or list of brands the consultant has worked for, and request references. Look for a consultant who has helped

businesses overcome the types of challenges you're facing or who has grown businesses very similar to yours and reach out to those companies to find out if they were satisfied with the service.

You say project management is not the key to success. Well, how can you manage an IT project without putting the emphasis on project management?

Put the emphasis on common sense. A great project manager who is tasked with executing a "mission impossible" will fail worse than a bad project manager because they will only extend the misery much in the same way that the skills of General Lee extended the duration of the U.S. Civil War, according to some historians. If your scope and timeline make sense, then even a mediocre project manager can deliver a successful outcome.

We're short staffed as it is. How can we free up key operational people to focus on a software implementation? That's impossible. The fact is that our employees are going to have to carve out a certain percentage of their time to work on the IT project. What's wrong with that approach?

The problem with involving the day-to-day managers and end-users in the IT system design is not only their lack of availability due to operational demands but more important, it is their lack of skill and experience in understanding and explaining what they do, how business workflows can be made efficient, and how data is structured in databases. They know their own tiny part in the process but rarely understand the big picture, nor do they understand or know about other more efficient ways of doing things which may be commonplace at other similar organizations.

*You will need to hire business analysts and embed them in your depart-
mental areas and then give them time to get up to speed on the pecu-
liarities of your business, prior to engaging an expensive consulting firm
to implement your new IT system. If you do not do this, then what will
happen is that the expensive consulting firm will not be able to get clear
requirements nor arrive at a good design. They will instead go round and
round in circles struggling to get the time and the attention of end-users
and when they finally do get their time and attention, they will be misled
by the end-users' lack of understanding of their own legacy systems and
lack of understanding of IT in general.*

As a C-Level I don't have time to think about how to phase in a software
implementation. I am busy running a company. This is why I hire IT consulting firms who specialize in implementing certain products. Why can't I
trust them to know how to create a realistic project plan?

*Objective, scope, and timeline cannot be defined without heavy C-Level
involvement because these IT projects are undertaken to fulfill a vision
put forth by the C-Levels. Furthermore, it is only the C-Levels that have
the authority to sign-off (or delegate someone else to sign-off) on an IT systems project which is a major undertaking for the organization in terms
of cost, risk, and impact. The consulting firm wants to win your business.
Oftentimes, to be awarded the contract, they will skew their advice to fit
what they think you want to hear.*

*As a C-Level it is up to you to get on the same page with your other
C-Level counterparts, and come up with a realistic, feasible, phased strategy to improve your IT systems slowly but surely. If you are the source of*

the unrealistic, impatient, flawed strategy, due to inattention or wishful thinking, then your lack of wisdom will flow downstream and make everybody else's job impossible and set hundreds if not thousands of people off on bad course that is doomed from the start. No matter how hard they work or how much they try, they will fail because of your bad leadership.

We are recruiting IT talent to staff our IT project. Isn't the most important thing to find somebody that has years of experience and who has built their career working exclusively with the exact software application that we are seeking to implement?

Someone who has years of experience with a particular software application and has done many implementations of that specific software package can add a certain level of insurance for the project. Normally the software developer company itself or one of their implementation partner firms will supply application specialists who have years of experience implementing that application and know it inside and out. But when hiring internally, the focus should be on other factors because otherwise you will limit yourself to a small pool of applicants for all the wrong reasons. The qualities you seek have more to do with common sense, creative thinking, written and oral communication, understanding how to optimize business processes, and the ability to get along with, mentor, and inspire coworkers than with extensive detailed knowledge of and experience with one specific software product.

Cast a wide net. The prize fish swims in many waters.

We plan to save big money by having our employees to do as much of the IT project as possible. The consulting firm doing our implementation charges high hourly rates. Our users are going to have a lot of homework on this IT project, and they just need to figure out how to squeeze that into their schedules. Why do you say that the users shouldn't have any homework, when after all, they know what they want and how things should work for them better than anyone else?

The composition of your internal project implementation team is a critical component to ensuring the success of the implementation. It is important that your approach to building an implementation team is aligned with your new system selection, general project planning, and accounts for several major internal and external factors.

The two biggest factors to consider throughout your IT project implementation team selection are the size and structure of your company, as well as the complexities of the project scope. The needs of the implementation project will dictate the roles and responsibilities necessary to ensure all components of the project are addressed. Meanwhile, the size and structure of your company will determine how these roles are identified and assigned. With these factors, designing an effective and efficient team must be strategic. To ensure the success of your IT project implementation, your team must be holistic and thus comprised of individuals from across the entire organization. It must also include any necessary external support. This includes senior executives, project managers, domain experts, end-users, and the implementation partner or vendor.

But don't think you can do everything by yourself with your in-house team even though they should contribute in important ways in many of the areas of the implementation. For most large IT projects, such as an ERP or CRM implementation, you will need an external partner. However, the problem is usually not an overemphasis on the internal team but an over reliance on the external partner. Building a strong internal team and taking much of the project in-house by hiring very skilled and experienced business analysts and possibly even functional and technical application specialists is a way to ensure quality, because those new hires can be free of day-to-day operational duties, focus on the project, and act as watchdogs to guard you against the external partner taking advantage of your ignorance and naivety. Also, new internal hires who are skilled business analysts have the skill to understand and communicate the requirements to the external partner, whereas your long-time in-the-trenches end-users will not know how to do that.

We want our users to have a very large say in the design of the new IT system. They understand our business the best. We need to have full participation with the users being involved in the design as much as possible. If the designers go away and design on their own, and users aren't able to talk freely because they are being interviewed instead of just brainstorming, won't that mean that the system gets designed without the user's needs being met?

End-users are users of applications. They don't design apps. They don't work on IT systems. They won't know what they don't know. End-users are busy and you shouldn't waste their time. Use business analysts working alongside functional application specialists to determine the requirements and to design and prototype solutions using an iterative approach. Bring in the end-users to kick the tires, not to design the car. Their involvement in vetting the solutions devised by others will take up plenty of their time. They will not complain about lack of participation. They are more likely to complain about the opposite.

If we backfill a role, such as hiring a new controller in our accounting department, so that we can free up the current controller to focus 100% on our ERP implementation project, what do we do when the project is over, and we no longer need two controllers?

If your organization is growing then new roles will open up for talented, dedicated, hardworking individuals. If your growth rate will not allow for the backfills to be perm hires, then consider long-term contracts that span the length of the project. Many of the most talented IT resources out there prefer to work on a contract basis for a variety of reasons.

Our C-levels and VP's are not agreeing on the next steps for our major IT digital transformation initiative. We had some missteps on our last major IT project are now we are trying to right the ship. How can we have a successful project when our top managers don't see eye to eye, and some of them are distancing themselves from the project?

Do not set out upon a long journey where members of your group are headed in different directions. Your team will end up scattered and vulnerable to capture by hostile forces.

We admit that the design meetings on our last software implementation project were less than optimal, but not letting our users speak their mind in our meetings is unacceptable. How can we let them participate and speak for as long as they wish to and about whatever they want but at the same time keep the meetings on track?

It's very important to involve users in the design phase since they have the most intimate understanding of current business processes; however, they have to be brought in at the right time, and that is not every single design meeting. Functional application specialists (usually consultants of the implementation partner) can interview business analysts study the legacy system, document the "as is" process, and then determine system requirements for the new IT system, after which business analysts and functional application specialists can go off and design prototypes for end-users to review and provide feedback on during separate meetings.

It's vital to have end-users participate in the design workshops where they can review and pass judgement on proposed designs that are presented to them, and get feedback from them at each iterative stage, as any confusion over how they will interact with or use the new system may impact its successful implementation, so the short answer is that we definitely need to let end-users participate in the design and feel comfortable speaking up to share their thoughts and concerns.

There are many methods to keep the meeting on the right track. One of the most effective ways, in our experience, is to physically point at an agenda. You should always share and post the agenda before the meeting and all participants can reference it at any time. When a conversation begins veering off-track, politely point at the activity or discussion in the agenda your meeting is currently focusing on and verbally remind everyone which topics are scheduled to be covered in the current meeting.

You say that the primary problem with IT systems design meetings is that the participants fail to think systematically and methodically but instead think episodically and anecdotally. Not sure I am getting this. Exactly what do you mean by this?

End-users tend to tell stories (episodes and anecdotes) about what goes on in their particular small piece of a much larger business process workflow. They don't understand what their coworkers do because they are on a "need-to-know" basis taking care of a very specific and small part of the assembly line. They can function perfectly well in day-to-day operations without a holistic understanding because they only need to handle a small part of the overall process.

But if you are trying to improve and optimize a business process, then you need to understand the whole process, because the tiny the part that the end-user wants to improve may turn out to be something that should be completely eliminated instead of improved. A business analyst, unlike an end-user, will systematically (looking at the whole system) and methodically (devising a method to achieve a high-level goal) go through each step of the business process in a logical order from step A to step Z, and therefore not miss any steps, and at the same time, will challenge the existing process because there may be a faster way from A to Z. The end-user may only be handling steps D through F. There may be a path from A directly to X, shortening the trip to Z, and eliminating steps D through F, or better yet, the entire process from A to Z may not be necessary because of another possibility that a business analyst, management consultant, or a functional application specialist may be aware of from working on other IT systems at other organizations.

The confusion arises in thinking that end-users have more to contribute than they actually do because typically, an end-user does have a tremendous amount of very detailed knowledge about steps D through F. What is ironic here is that steps D through F are not needed anymore, so the end-user's knowledge although vast, is totally useless. Discovering this kind of useless information is very common occurrence when you systematically and methodically analyze a typical business process workflow that has evolved over a period of years to become a mission critical part of an organization's daily operations.

Our IT design meetings have a moderator, they follow a set agenda, and we have a "parking lot" to keep the meeting topics from going off on tangents. But somehow, our meetings are still not very productive as far as coming up with concrete results. What are we missing?

Avoid meetings. Do not have meetings for the sake of having meetings. If your staff spends all their time attending meetings, they will not be productive. Unnecessary meetings can lead to tasks being left incomplete or forgotten due to time constraints. Keep meetings short and relevant if you must have them. The biggest waste of time is dragging everyone into all the design meetings. End-users aren't designers. They should not have to attend all the design meetings. In general, they should only attend the feedback sessions.

IT design decisions must be carefully evaluated for their financial impact and efficiency gains. How can you say that most IT design decisions are just a matter of personal preference and that it doesn't really matter what you decide? Surely, that must be wrong.

This confusion arises because major decisions do have a huge financial impact and of course, they should be evaluated from a financial perspective and measured in dollars and cents and taken very seriously. However, most of the decisions on an IT project are minor decisions that have no financial impact. So, most of the decision points are just a matter of arbitrary personal preference. Nonetheless, stalling on these petty decisions can derail your IT project. Although these decisions are minor, they must be made, because the new system cannot be stood up until the decisions are made and the system is configured for that decision.

Delaying minor, petty, inconsequential decisions is not merely pointless, or merely foolish, it is crippling.

At our organization we instill a sense of teamwork and mutual respect in all our employees. It's important for us to work as a team. In designing our new IT system, all stakeholders should participate equally in the design. How can you say that IT design is not a team sport or that it is not a communal activity?

The implementation of a new system, whether it's an ERP or CRM or other solution, is a long process that hinges on several factors and involves many people. The input of your organization will be required to coordinate and manage the implementation internally while ensuring that expectations and concerns are communicated properly with your partner so that everyone is on the same wavelength. As such, you will be required to work in teams throughout the project, be it with your main implementation partner or with third-party providers, or even internally with your colleagues. Teamwork during the project implementation is thus vital to the success and to ensure that you obtain a solution that meets and even exceeds your objectives.

Not only is teamwork important to collaborate and communicate properly, but it's also stimulating and motivating and even fun. As the implementation of your new system is a large-scale project, it's normal to expect challenges and unforeseen events. This makes it even more important to overcome challenges as a team, both internally and externally. By leveraging the different strengths of your team members, you will be able to identify aspects to be improved and quickly find solutions. New possibilities can also emerge from discussing and sharing different points of view. This way, results can even exceed your expectations. Moreover, teamwork fosters a climate of loyalty and respect where everyone's strengths, skills and input are valued, making for a rewarding and enriching experience. Striving for a common objective, in this case the launch of a new system, helps keep everyone motivated even during the more trying phases of the project. You will increase your team's productivity and efficiency. You will also reduce the risk of the same errors reoccurring by exchanging with others and learning from the experience.

Now, having said all that, on a team, say for example a baseball team, there is a catcher, a pitcher, a shortstop, and so on. The catcher does not run into the outfield to catch a flyball, but rather stays behind home plate. An end-user should be in design review meetings. This point is emphasized over and over again in this book for a reason. It is perhaps the most misunderstood aspect of IT system design. We want to include end-users, but we must include them only at the appropriate moments and in the appropriate way. A professional IT systems designer should be guiding the conversation during requirements gathering and discovery sessions. They should also be getting the end-user's feedback on prototypes that were designed and built by professional IT systems designers. So, the end-user is part of the design process, but their involvement is limited and focused correctly on activities they are able to perform properly.

You seem to stress the importance of having solid evidence of progress on IT projects to be able to tell whether the project is on track. Isn't the only real evidence working software, as Agile principles say?

No. Real evidence can also be write-ups. Working software is built off of design documents in the same way that a house is constructed from blueprints and engineering schematics. Of course, you could have programmers code apps without any documentation, and it is done all the time. It is a sloppy and irresponsible way of working which leads to rework, difficulty in maintaining the code in the future, and misalignment between requirements and functionality. Skipping the design documentation saves time in the short run but wastes time in the long run, and results in poor quality work.

How can we ensure that our IT systems design meetings result in good designs?

Well, there is no single answer for this, but I will share some of my past experiences which have helped make design meetings more efficient and productive.
- Good planning - Well run and effective meetings require a lot of planning. A typical meeting model is: 10% Planning; 80% Meeting; 10% Follow-up. A much more effective model is 50% Planning; 20% Meeting; 30% Follow-up.

- Focus on the objectives and desired outcomes of the meeting. Agree with the meeting owner where things are now and where you want to go. Second, consider the people: who needs to be there and what they bring, group dynamics, participation, and possible resistance.
- Purpose, People, Process and Progress - Design your meeting with these questions in mind: "How will we know if this meeting is successful?" "Who really needs to be at this meeting"? "How are we going to make it work?" "What have we learned as a result of this meeting"?
- Having the right stakeholders in the meeting - Invite the minimum number of people needed to accomplish your objectives. Determine what role each person must play. Look for opportunities to get some people's input ahead of the meeting so that your session has the smallest number of critical participants.
- Consider post-meeting collaboration as part of your meeting plan - a) Allow people to get information from the meeting even if they're not there and b) Allow people to continue good conversations and connections they establish at the face-to-face meeting (e.g., online discussion topics, conference calls).

Agile principles call for less documentation, not more of it. Getting bogged down in lots of documentation was part of the old way of doing things that didn't work. How can you be emphasizing documentation as a solution to wasteful IT spending these days?

Good documents are always useful and needed regardless of the implementation methodology, either Agile or waterfall. If you recall, a traditional approach to IT projects always defines and documents requirements first before the system is being implemented, and while Agile development methodology was created as an alternative to this documentation-driven development process, it did not set out to eliminate the documentation completely. It simply placed more value on working on the system and solution than on comprehensive documentation because of the dynamic nature of system implementation. So, there is nothing in the Agile development methodology that inherently prevents us from creating as much documentation as the project requires. There are, in fact, situations in which documentation is absolutely required. Adding user stories to the backlog, creating flowcharts, drafting wireframes, documenting client meetings, are all standard aspects of Agile. Agile simply suggests being smart about it. Documentation should be "just barely good enough". Too much or overly comprehensive documentation would be a waste of time, and developers rarely trust detailed documentation anyway because it's usually out of sync with the actual code. On the other hand, experience shows that too little documentation is always a source of problems with team communication, learning, and knowledge sharing.

In this fast-paced world, people no longer have the time to write or read long detailed documents. We need to build working applications and test them in a sandbox environment and in conference room pilots. Why can't we skip the documents and move straight into the prototypes? Isn't that what Agile principles are urging us to do?

No. We cannot skip the documents and move straight into the prototypes directly. The Agile principles recommend streamlined documentation but that does not mean we will not need any documentation. The creation and maintenance of documentation is a "necessary evil" to some and an enjoyable task for others. Either way, there are several valid reasons to invest time in it:

- Your project stakeholders require it. The creation of documentation is fundamentally a business decision, you are investing the resources of the project stakeholders in the development of the documentation, so they should have a say on whether their money is to be spent that way.

- To support communication with an external group. It isn't always possible to co-locate a development team and it isn't always possible to always have project stakeholders available. Shared documentation is often part of the solution in combination with occasional face-to-face discussions, teleconferencing, email, and collaborative tools.

- To support organizational memory. One of the principles of Agile Modeling is "Enabling the next effort is your secondary goal", which is meant as a counterbalance to the principle "Working software is your primary goal". That means that while you need to develop software, you also need to develop the supporting documentation required to use, operate, support, and maintain it over time.

- For audit purposes. Depending on the type of system you are developing, it might fall under certain audit guidelines. In that case, you would need to follow a defined process and capture proof that you did so, resulting in more documentation. However, if you really dig into what compliance requires, lightweight documentation usually works just fine.

- To think something through. The act of putting ideas down on paper can help you solidify them and discover problems with your thinking. What appears clear and straightforward in your mind can often prove to be very complicated once you attempt to describe it in detail, and you can often benefit from writing it down first.

We store all our IT project documents in a project folder on SharePoint. It always seems to get disorganized, and we are never quite sure which documents are obsolete and which are still relevant. How do we solve this problem?

The answer is less weed and more weeding.

We have standard templates for all our technical specifications and other IT-related documents. We maintain strict standards which ensures consistency. Why would you advise us to have lax standards? How could that possibly help us?

The spider lies in wait as the dragon fly soars. Neither go hungry.

Each author should have the freedom to tailor their documentation in a manner that suits their own individual style. Yes, it is wise to establish documentation standards which are the rules that guide the creation and distribution of documents within your team or organization and to use the standard documentation templates. And yes, there are many benefits of using standard documentation templates including ensuring clarity and consistency by helping the author provide the right level of detail and to ensure that they cover the typically important topics. While it is true that your team needs clear, up-to-date, documentation to help all members stay informed, be more efficient, and communicate clearly, because enforcing too rigid a policy is counter-productive.

It's very hard to gauge whether the documents being created during the IT project are any good. We have to rely upon the consultants. We have to trust that they know how detailed those documents need to be and whether they are accurate or useful. Surely, you can't expect us to peer review the documents created by consultants or to expect us to tell them how many and what kind of documents they need to produce?

This is a discipline. Embrace this discipline and wed it to your heart. I have yet to meet a person who gets excited about creating documentation on a software project regardless of whether it is ERP or CRM or any IT project for that matter. It generally falls into the same category as tracking time. When everyone is so busy doing the work, they don't see the reason for documenting what's being done. Documentation provides a record as to the why, what, and how behind decisions, development, and implementation. Documentation on projects should never be negotiable; it is for the benefit of all parties including the client, users, vendor, and the partners. Many types of project documentation should be created depending on the size and complexity of the project, and every consultant should know what documentation needs to be created during the journey of the project. Here are some basic document types you should always have regardless of the size of the project:

- Future State Business Process (Expected Benefits, Goals, Scope)
- Business Requirements Document (BRD)
- Functional Design & Technical Design Documents
- Test Cases
- Training Materials (User Guides)
- And more…

We would love to think that our employees will stick around forever and be able to regurgitate the complex details of lengthy discussions years later. The reality is that the human brain is not a hard drive.

Shine the bright light of knowledge into the darkness of a murky future with concise, lucid documentation.

Excel workbooks with rows of unexplained data are insufficient. We need prose. Imagine if this book were rows in an Excel spreadsheet. Would you understand any of the important concepts were are imparting to you?

Our IT staff is stretched very thin and works at maximum capacity. Some employees haven't had a vacation in years. They barely have time to do the configurations and setups, so how can we demand that they document all their work, and then add to that by asking them to peer review the documentation of other IT team members? Don't you realize that this is totally unrealistic?

Reverse engineering is the reverse of what we want to do. Trudging through the snowy woods stumbling into our own frozen tracks and ruts to find out where we have left off is the path of the fool. Leave clearly visible markers along the trail, not breadcrumbs to be scattered by the winds or eaten by the crows.

If some of our IT team members are having trouble creating good design documents, we need to mentor them so that they can get better at it. We have a commitment to training and developing the careers of our employees. We don't fire or kick people off projects. We give them the training and tools to succeed. You seem to be advising us to get rid of people that can't write good design documents. How can we do such a thing?

The house, the blueprint, and the architect are one. From one good architect a mighty fortress arises. Find her at the height of her powers.

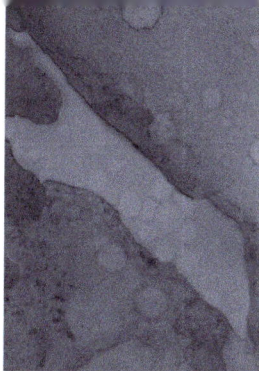

Author Bios

Andy Cheng

Andy Cheng who hails from Shanghai, is a partner with a Big Four business software implementation practice based in Manhattan, combining technical expertise, functional design acumen, and philosophical wisdom to guide IT projects into balanced alignment.

Renato Bellu

Ren Bellu is an accountant, computer programmer, management consultant and out-of-the-box thinker who specializes in digital transformation and IT project turnarounds. Ren is the author of Microsoft Dynamics 365 for Dummies among other titles. Ren lives in South Jersey near Philadelphia, Pennsylvania.

Hoag Holmgren

Hoag Holmgren is a fully sanctioned Zen teacher and author of No Better Place: a New Zen Primer. He lives in Colorado and is the founder of Mountain Path Sangha, a Zen practice community that meets online and in person. His newsletter ZEN SUN WEEKLY ships every Sunday.

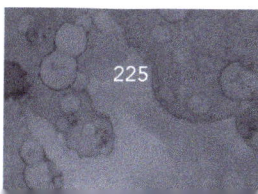

Wake Up!

Join the Zen of IT Revolution!

This book focuses on the correct philosophical approach toward the selection, implementation, configuration, adoption, and continuous process improvement of the apps that comprise the core business software of your organization.

Contained within these pages are the deep insights the authors have gained from the study and practice of Zen and from decades of direct involvement in IT projects of all types and sizes, within a wide variety of industries including educational institutions, public sector, not-for-profit, hospitals and clinics, technology startups, family-owned businesses, distributors, manufacturers, consulting firms, staffing companies, and large publicly traded multi-national corporations.

Andy Cheng, a Partner / Principal with a Big Four Global Services Organization based in Manhattan, leads a top-tier business software implementation practice.

Ren Bellu, author of *Microsoft Dynamics 365 for Dummies*, is an accountant, computer programmer, management consultant and out-of-the-box thinker who specializes in digital transformation and IT project turnarounds.

Hoag Holmgren is a fully sanctioned Zen teacher and author of *No Better Place: a New Zen Primer*.

9 798822 957633